A History of
the U.S. Men's
National Soccer Team

A History of
the U.S. Men's
National Soccer Team

Clemente A. Lisi

ROWMAN & LITTLEFIELD
Lanham • Boulder • New York • London

Published by Rowman & Littlefield
A wholly owned subsidary of The Rowman & Littlefield Publishing Group, Inc.
4501 Forbes Boulevard, Suite 200, Lanham, Maryland 20706
www.rowman.com

Unit A, Whitacre Mews, 26-34 Stannary Street, London SE11 4AB

British Library Cataloguing in Publication Information Available

Library of Congress Cataloging-in-Publication Data
Names: Lisi, Clemente Angelo, 1975– author.
Title: A history of the U.S. men's national soccer team / Clemente A. Lisi.
Other titles: History of the United States men's national soccer team
Description: Lanham, Maryland : Rowman & Littlefield, 2017. | Includes
    bibliographical references and index. |
Identifiers: LCCN 2017005972 (print) | LCCN 2017027865 (ebook) | ISBN
    9781442277588 (electronic) | ISBN 9781442277571 (hardcover : alk. paper)
Subjects: LCSH: United States Men's National Soccer Team—History. |
    Soccer—United States—History.
Classification: LCC GV944.U5 (ebook) | LCC GV944.U5 L57 2017 (print) | DDC
    796.334/630973—dc23
LC record available at https://lccn.loc.gov/2017005972

∞™ The paper used in this publication meets the minimum requirements of
American National Standard for Information Sciences—Permanence of Paper
for Printed Library Materials, ANSI/NISO Z39.48-1992.

Printed in the United States of America

*To those who work hard every day to
help soccer grow in the United States*

Contents

Contents

Acknowledgments

This book would have never been possible if not for the love and support of so many people. First of all, thank you to my wonderful wife Kate, for her unrelenting love, and to my children, Grace and Mark, who continue to make me see the world with the wonder and curiosity only a child can bring. Thanks again to my editors at Rowman & Littlefield. I have worked with them since writing my first book in 2007, and it has been a great relationship. They saw the need for soccer books long before they became fashionable. A special thanks to my editor Christen Karniski for her insight, patience, and hard work.

I would also like to take the time to thank J Hutcherson of USSoccer-Players.com, who has given me the chance to cover American soccer for the past decade. This book would also not have been possible without the hard work and dedication of so many historians and journalists who came before me. They served as an inspiration to me throughout this process. My thanks, in particular, go to U.S. Soccer for providing me with vital statistics and Ed Farnsworth for compiling every box score of every U.S. game. His work, and that of the Society of American Soccer History, has been instrumental in keeping the history of this great game alive.

A special thank you goes to those who helped bring to life the words on these pages with their photography. I would like to single out ISI Photos, as well as Jon van Woerden for his support and generosity.

Introduction

If there ever was a team that galvanized a nation, it has been the U.S. men's national soccer team. The 1980 "Miracle on Ice" hockey team gave Americans something to cheer about during the Cold War. The 1992 Dream Team showed the world U.S. basketball dominance. And the 1999 U.S. team that won the Women's World Cup highlighted the equality achieved by women in sports. But the U.S. men's soccer team has done this on a more consistent basis.

The team did it in 1990, making history after qualifying for the World Cup for the first time in 40 years. It happened again four years later, when the United States hosted the World Cup. Once again, in 2002, Americans awoke in the middle of the night to watch the team reach the World Cup quarterfinals half a world away in South Korea. Then came 2010 and 2014, when millions were enthralled by a team that was able to captivate a nation, pushing soccer more and more into the American sports mainstream. And to think, it was not until 1984 that a national team game was broadcast on television in the United States.

But this was not always the case. The national team toiled in obscurity for decades, at a time when soccer did not get mainstream media coverage. The team itself struggled to win games, playing like the chips were down—and for many years they were. The Americans were the underdogs both in their own region and at the international level, going 40 years without qualifying for a World Cup, before finally breaking through in 1989. Since then, the team has been on an upswing, putting together many gritty performances, while also putting together some shocking upsets.

A History of the U.S. Men's National Soccer Team recounts some of those history-making—and other obscure, but also significant—feats. From its historic 1991 Gold Cup final victory, to its showing at the 1995 Copa America, to reaching the 2009 Confederations Cup final, the U.S. men's national soccer team has not only aided in the game's growth, but also helped turn the United States into a soccer nation.

Like all my books, this one aims to both inform and entertain. Older fans will revel in the nostalgia and player profiles; younger ones will learn about tournaments and games that have long been forgotten but were nonetheless important to the team's growth. I hope this book will serve as a reference as the United States prepares for the 2018 World Cup and for years to come.

1

Humble Beginnings: 1916–1929

The story of the U.S. men's national soccer team started in 1916, on a field in Stockholm. It was there that the Americans played their first official game against Sweden—a match the Americans won, 3–2, after accepting an invitation to play in the Scandinavian nation. The team's creation came three years after the United States Football Association (USFA) had been formed on April 5, 1913, after the official charter was signed at the Astor House Hotel in New York City. Until then, the game had been played largely on an amateur basis—and had even featured teams that had represented the United States—but the creation of a national governing body was meant to professionalize the game, as had been done in England.

At the same time, the National Challenge Cup, a national soccer tournament for all clubs now known as the Lamar Hunt U.S. Open Cup, was played in the 1913–1914 season. Brooklyn Field Club won the first title, a trophy donated by Thomas Dewar, for the purpose of trying to promote the sport. Dewar, a famous Scottish whisky distiller, was a big fan of the game and had donated various trophies for sports tournaments in the United States and Great Britain. The competition was the first truly national soccer competition at a time when most leagues and tournaments were regional. It remains the oldest cup competition in the United States.

The U.S.–Sweden game, part of a six-match tour, also included a trip to Norway. The USFA, the precursor to the modern-day United States Soccer Federation (or as it is commonly known, U.S. Soccer), had been created in 1913, with the task of overseeing the sport throughout the country. Soccer was growing before World War I. The American Soccer

Photo 1.1. The U.S. national team poses for a photo in 1916 during a tour of Scandinavia. (National Soccer Hall of Fame Archive)

League (ASL), which formed in 1921, was the first professional league in the United States. The ASL attracted players countrywide—and even from Europe—and helped boost the game's popularity at a time when baseball and horse racing were the most beloved spectator sports. The team featured captain Thomas Swords, a forward who played for the Fall River Rovers of the New England League. The first national team was comprised primarily of players from the Northeast, recruited for the purpose of playing for what was called the All-American Soccer Football Team. Swords, whose energetic style and rugged athleticism typified the American game at the time, would go on to score the first-ever goal for the United States. Following the tour, he would never again feature for the United States.

Thomas Cahill, who served as the first USFA secretary general and head coach, led a 14-man roster that featured players from teams in Massachusetts, Missouri, New York, New Jersey, and Pennsylvania. Cahill is considered one of the founding fathers of American soccer and a tireless champion for the sport in the country. Born in New York City, he moved to St. Louis—one of the country's soccer centers at the time, along with Newark, New Jersey, and Fall River, Massachusetts—and became involved as an amateur sports administrator, most notably of track and baseball. Cahill only became interested in soccer after attending a game that featured a local side playing a team visiting from Toronto. He founded and managed the St. Louis Shamrocks, a name that honored his Irish heritage, who competed in the St. Louis Association Foot Ball League. The team won the title in 1899 and 1900. In 1910, Cahill moved to Newark, with the aim of establishing a national soccer body to oversee the game. He finally achieved his goal in 1913, and was named U.S. coach in 1916.

At the same time, Cahill was editor of Spalding's annual *Official Soccer Football Guide* from 1912 to 1924. He sent a letter to soccer officials in Sweden that also contained the guide in 1916, and took them at their word when they proposed that the Americans send a team to tour the country. Cahill jumped at the chance. He had attended the FIFA Congress in Sweden in 1912, and saw the potential in having a team representing the United States play abroad.

Europe was under siege at the time, as World War I raged on. The United States was still neutral at this point in the conflict, as were the Scandinavian countries. It was little surprise that the first U.S. tour abroad brought them to Sweden for what would be a seven-week trip. The American team received favorable reviews. The *Brooklyn Daily Eagle* raved that the roster "is about as good a combination as could reasonably be expected to make the trip and will without doubt give a good account of itself."

It did just that in its first game against Sweden, on August 20, in front of 16,000 spectators in Stockholm. Also present was King Gustav V. In light rain, forwards Harry Cooper and Charles Ellis both scored, along with Swords, for the United States. Carl Linde, a prominent Swedish sportswriter at the time, noted that the Americans represented a "new way of playing" soccer and that the style could be best described as "primitive brutality," according to the book *Soccer in a Football World* by Dave Wangerin.

Indeed, the Swedes, who had established a team as early as 1908, did not take the defeat well. The Americans' sojourn in Sweden also included nonofficial games versus local teams—four matches that were not considered "full internationals" because they did not involve opponents who were national teams represented as a FIFA member nation. But they still constituted a good test for the newly assembled squad. One such game played in Gothenburg, a 2–1 victory against Orgryte, led to fan violence. Fans of the local club attacked several American players after the final whistle. Goalkeeper George Tintle was pinned to a fence and kicked by fans, while Ellis punched one fan on his way to the dressing room. The violence didn't end there. On his way to the team hotel, one fan jumped into Cahill's car and attempted to steal a U.S. flag. The *Brooklyn Daily Eagle* reported that Cahill leaped out of his car to stop the assailant:

> Calling to the chauffer to stop, Cahill leaped out, and pursuing the vandal, delivered some well-aimed blows with his cane. He was making good headway toward the complete annihilation of his opponent when policemen with drawn swords interfered and drove Cahill back. The crowd gathered again, and the Americans were lucky to make their escape.

King Gustav, upon hearing the news, ordered a special investigation into the matter, but nothing came of it. Instead, the Americans and Swedes turned the series of games into a cultural exchange. Although soccer was their game, the U.S. team also showed locals the game of baseball, and the hosts later introduced the sport in various Stockholm schools. At the same time, reported Wangerin, the hosts reimbursed the Americans $6,500 for living expenses, and the players divided $1,000 between them.

The Americans moved on to Norway. It was on September 3, in front of a crowd of 25,000, in Oslo, that the All-Americans, as they were better known, played Norway to a 1–1 draw in the second official international match of the tour. Ellis scored the lone goal for the Americans. He would end up staying behind once the tour came to an end, accepting a $50-a-week job to coach the Stockholm soccer team. For his part, Cahill called the match the "fastest and most exciting" of the tour, Wangerin reported.

Photo 1.2. Astor House in New York City served as the first headquarters of U.S. Soccer. (Library of Congress)

Overall, Cahill also deemed the tour a success, but he acknowledged that the Americans had generally been outclassed by the Swedes regardless of the results. "It was American grit, pluck, and endurance that won," Wangerin reported Cahill as saying. "No great football stars were members of our team, but we had the pluckiest aggregation ever banded together."

WORLD WAR I

World War I brought soccer to a standstill throughout most of the world. Teams were unable to travel to Europe, where the fighting was taking place, and many players in the various leagues throughout the country had been drafted into the war. The national team program remained inactive for eight years. Despite this, the Roaring Twenties were good for the sport domestically. The ASL's formation, which took place with the help of deep-pocketed investors, was helpful in creating organized soccer in Europe, but a dispute arose with the USFA concerning foreign players breaking their contracts in Europe to play in the United States. That issue, compounded by the fight between the USFA and the ASL regarding revenue-sharing among touring foreign clubs, led to the "American Soccer War." The ASL would cease to exist in 1933, a few years after the start of the Great Depression. It would be the first of many U.S. pro leagues to collapse in the 20th century.

1924 OLYMPICS

The Americans had not participated in the 1920 Olympics, but the USFA was determined to participate four years later. Missing out on the Antwerp Games caused friction between Gus Manning, the first president of the USFA, and Cahill, who claimed that only $149 had been raised of the $10,000 needed to fund the trip. Cahill was fired, and the team was coached by George H. Burford. His claim to fame had been working as the physical director of the Pennsylvania Railroad YMCA, while also working to introduce soccer in Boston's public schools. The USFA put together its team after soliciting nominations from club officials, coaches, and journalists. A series of tryouts and exhibitions led to a final roster.

Nonetheless, the players who were chosen were not the best the country had to offer. Only one player—goalkeeper Jimmy Douglas—played in the ASL. For the USFA, the goal was to field amateur players in strict accordance with International Olympic Committee rules; however, it had become increasingly difficult for FIFA to determine who was an amateur. It varied from country to country, but the United States made it clear—only players who did not receive payment for playing.

The team, which featured amateur players, traveled to Paris for the Summer Games and opened with a 1–0 victory on May 24, against Estonia, at Pershing Park, in front of 10,000 spectators. Andy Stradan tallied the winning goal in a very physical affair. The American style of play was not much different than what had been seen a decade earlier in Sweden. The second game played by the United States, on May 29, resulted in an early elimination from the tournament—a 3–0 loss to mighty Uruguay, the eventual gold-medal winners. Uruguay's definition of amateur was radically different from the U.S. version. The *New York Times* heaped praise on Uruguay, saying, "No other team [at the Olympics] has shown anything like the same mastery of the game."

After the Olympics, the team continued to tour Europe. The Americans earned a 3–2 victory against Poland in Warsaw on June 10, but were defeated by Ireland, 3–1, six days later in Dublin. In 1925, the team played only two full internationals, both versus Canada, which were part of a move to create a regular U.S.–Canada series similar to what had transpired in Europe decades earlier between England and Scotland. The plan never took hold. After losing, 1–0, in Montreal on June 27, the Americans trounced Canada, 6–1, on November 8, at Ebbets Field in Brooklyn, New York, in the team's first home game. Archie Stark scored four goals, and Davey Brown added

ARCHIE STARK

Archibald "Archie" Stark was born on December 21, 1897, in Glasgow, Scotland, and died on May 27, 1985, in Kearny, New Jersey. He was one of the country's best soccer players during the 1920s and 1930s, and a dominant striker who would go on to be one of the ASL's biggest stars.

Career: Stark moved to the United States at age 13, settling in northern New Jersey. At the time, Hudson County was a hotbed of Scottish immigrants, a place where soccer thrived as the most popular sport among expats. That's where Stark and his brother Tommy, a defender, got their starts. At just 14, Stark turned pro, playing with the Scottish Americans of the National Association Football League (NAFL). In 1915, the team won the American Cup, defeating Boston Celtic, 1–0, on a Stark goal. In 1917, following a move to Babcock & Wilcox, a team based in Bayonne, New Jersey, Stark joined the U.S. Army and served during World War I. Following stints with several NAFL clubs, he defected to the ASL, signing with the New York Field Club. In 1924, he joined Bethlehem Steel, one of the best ASL teams at the time and home to several Scottish-born players. In his first season, Stark solidified his reputation as a prolific scorer, tallying 67 goals in 44 games. In 1926, Bethlehem Steel won the National Challenge Cup (now known as the U.S. Open Cup), defeating Ben Millers in the final. Stark scored a hat trick in a 7–2 rout. Bethlehem went on to win the ASL title in 1927 and 1929. It also won the Eastern Soccer League title that same year. The team folded in 1930, and Stark signed with the Fall River (Massachusetts) Marksmen, taking part in a tour of Europe. He played with the Newark Americans during the 1930–1931 season. In 1933, Stark ended up playing with Kearny Irish of the ASL. The team won the title, and Stark's 22 goals made him the top scorer, an honor he shared with Razzo Carroll of the Kearny Scots. Stark was inducted into the U.S. National Soccer Hall of Fame in 1950.

National Team: Stark earned only two caps with the United States, both in games against Canada in 1925. In his first game, Canada defeated the United States, 1–0. In the second game, Stark tallied four goals, as the Americans won, 6–1. Stark was invited to play on the World Cup team in 1930, but he declined the offer. Instead, he was interested in "looking for a new livelihood and trying to get an automotive business started in Kearny. By the time of the Fall River tour of Czechoslovakia, Hungary, and Austria in August and September, the business was up and running, and he was able to take time off from it," according to the Society for American Soccer History.

Photo 1.3.   Archie Stark (center) while battling two players during his time with Beth-lehem Steel. (U.S. Soccer)

two for the lopsided win. A year later, the United States did one better, again defeating Canada at Ebbetts Field on November 6, by a score of 6–2. Any plan for an annual series ended there. It would also be the only international the United States would play that year.

1928 OLYMPICS

The USFA, determined not to miss out on a major international tournament, sent a team to the 1928 Olympics in Amsterdam. Burford was again the coach/trainer, while Elmer Schroeder served as manager. But the roster had been thrown together at the last minute, and the team arrived in the Netherlands without having played a single scrimmage. The United States took on Argentina on May 29, in front of 4,000 fans, losing, 11–2. Despite losing a player to injury in the second half and being forced to play a man short, Argentina never stopped attacking. The Americans were one and done, the ouster coming in humiliating fashion at Olympic Stadium in the first round of the single-elimination tournament. U.S. goalkeeper Albert Cooper, who worked as an apprentice stage electrician for the Metropolitan Opera in New York, let in all the goals that day and was left reeling after an early shot on goal left him in a semiconscious state. But the *St. Louis Post-Dispatch* did not fault Cooper or his teammates for the loss:

> Thrown together from various sections of the United States, sent aboard ship without even one practice game to weld them together, managed by a man who apparently did not know his stuff . . . our puny, half-backed outfit was doomed in advance. Until America changes its "amateur" definition to conform to European standards we cannot hope to battle on even terms.

Argentina would win the silver medal behind its rival Uruguay. The United States would have two years to prepare for the inaugural World Cup, a place where it could compete on more even terms with the world's best teams. With the ASL firmly established as the country's professional league, the federation had a place with a fertile player pool. Manning and Cahill, who served as the USFA secretary at the time, agreed that sending a team to the 1930 World Cup was a priority even though it needed the host nation to underwrite the U.S. squad's travel expenses.

2

Early World Cup Success: 1930–1949

The 1930 World Cup, the first soccer tournament designed by FIFA and its then-president, Jules Rimet, to determine a global champion, was to be played in Uruguay, home to the defending Olympic champion. The tournament would ultimately feature 13 teams. There was no qualification process—the only time such a thing would happen—and all of FIFA's members were invited. South American nations gladly accepted (the proximity to Uruguay's capital, Montevideo, certainly helped), but European countries were more skeptical given the cost and burden that would come with a transatlantic boat trip.

1930 WORLD CUP

The United States sailed to Uruguay after departing from Hoboken, New Jersey, on the SS *Munargo* and trained aboard the vessel until they arrived on July 1, 1930, following an 18-day voyage that included stops in the Brazilian cities of Rio de Janeiro and Santos. The *Munargo* was both a commercial and passenger ship that had been built in 1921, and traveled mainly between New York City and Miami. In later years, the vessel was acquired by the U.S. Navy and used to move troops to Northern Europe during World War II—and as a hospital vessel in 1943—until it was taken out of commission in 1946.

The U.S. national team at the time was comprised of six British-born players, although only one—George Moorhouse—had played professionally, with the Tranmere Rovers. Moorehouse, however, was no ringer.

Photo 2.1.   The U.S. team traveled on the S.S. *Munargo* for the 1930 World Cup in Uruguay. (Library of Congress)

He'd played just two games for the English club, at the time in the third division, some eight years earlier. The others, from Scotland, had moved to the United States as either children or teenagers. None of them had ever played in Britain. Physically fit, the team would eventually be nicknamed the "shot-putters" because of their size. In all three of its games, the United States featured the same lineup: goalkeeper Jimmy Douglas (New York Nationals), right back Alexander "Alec" Wood (Detroit Holley Carburetor), left back Bart McGhee (New York Nationals), center back Raphael Tracey (St. Louis Ben Millers), left halfback Andy Auld (Providence Gold Bugs), inside left and captain Tom Florie (New Bedford Whalers), center forward Bert Patenaude (Fall River Marksmen), inside right Billy Gonsalves (Fall River Marksmen), and outside right James Brown (New York Giants). Everyone except Moorhouse and Tracey hailed from the ASL.

The 14-player roster was chosen through a series of tryout games. As noted soccer writer Brian Glanville stated in his book *The Story of the World Cup*, the American players were known for "their strong defense and breakaway attacks." It had been 14 years since the tour of Sweden and Norway, but the American style of play, as typified by the ASL at the time, still put a huge emphasis on rugged play and physical fitness. The team also shored up its defense—the 11–2 loss to Argentina still weighed heavily on those at the federation—in the hopes it could surprise its more technical and experienced European and South American opponents.

Once in Montevideo, organizers split the teams into four groups. The United States was placed in Group 4, with Belgium and Paraguay. The team benefitted from having players in the ASL—widely considered one of the best domestic leagues in the world at the time—a result of the high level of soccer being played in the St. Louis Soccer League and National Challenge Cup (the original name of the U.S. Open Cup). Indeed, the ASL's fall-to-spring schedule made it so that the players were accustomed to the damp and chilly conditions of a South American winter.

The Americans were essentially coached by the Irish-born John "Jack" Coll, who had moved to the United States in 1922, and Robert Millar. Also part of the process of choosing the roster had been Wilfred Cummings, who had served as the USFA's treasurer since 1921, and acted as the team's general manager in Uruguay. Millar had played for St. Mirren in Scotland and moved to the United States, eventually playing and coaching in the ASL. Coll, meanwhile, served as the team's physical trainer and ensured the players adhered to a strict fitness regimen during the trip to Uruguay. Coll had successfully trained several ASL clubs, notably the New York Giants, and brought a wealth of experience to the team bench.

In the opener against Belgium on July 13, at Estadío Parque Central in Montevideo, the Americans cruised to a 3–0 win in front of 18,000 fans. Goals from McGhee, Florie, and Patenaude sunk Belgium. Born in Scotland, McGhee moved to Philadelphia at age 13, to live with his father, a former Scottish forward who had played with Hibernian and Celtic. Patenaude scored the game's final goal. He would go on to score a hat trick, the first in World Cup history, in the following game four days later against Paraguay, also at Estadío Parque Central, in what resulted in another 3–0 victory in front of a crowd of just 800.

With a 2–0 record, the United States had won the group—to the surprise of many—and advanced to the semifinals, where Argentina awaited them. The *New York Times* published the following headline after the victory: "U.S. Favorite to Win World Soccer's Title." In another article, the newspaper boldly extolled the team's talents, writing, "The United States team, because of its splendid showing in the tourney, is favored to carry off the world's championship." But its semifinal opponent, Argentina, would again prove too much for the team to handle.

On July 26, at the Estadío Centenario, playing in front of an estimated crowd of 80,000, Argentina was too strong for the Americans. Subs were not allowed at the time. Thus, the United States was forced to play with 10 men after Tracey broke his leg in the first half. Down 1–0 at halftime, Argentina scored five goals in the second half to win the game, 6–1. Guillermo Stabile of Argentina, who would finish the tournament as top scorer with eight goals, scored twice against the Americans that day.

Uruguay would eventually defeat Argentina in the final to maintain its global dominance.

The *New York Times*, so high on the U.S. team on the eve of the match, was not shy about its feeling that soccer may not be a game for American athletes. The newspaper said, "It's more natural for an American . . . to use a stick or implement in his hands than it is to depend on his feet or his head." As for the Americans, dark times lay ahead following the collapse of the ASL and the World Cup's move to Europe. The ASL, which at the time rivaled the NFL in terms of fan engagement and was only second to baseball, would fall victim to the "Soccer Wars" and the Great Depression. The league had boycotted the Challenge Cup in 1928, but when three teams defied that order, the ASL suspended them. The USFA and FIFA declared the ASL an "outlaw league," which led the federation to bankroll a rival league. The creation of the Eastern Professional Soccer League (ESL) resulted in the defection of many ASL clubs, crippling the league. The ESL and ASL merged for the 1929–1930 season, but the damage had been done.

The ASL collapsed in 1933, and the idea that the USFA would conspire with FIFA, a European-based sports governing body, led to the image that soccer was a sport controlled by foreigners. Soccer's popularity declined, and the sport was relegated to minor-league status. The ASL returned in 1933, with fewer teams, mostly on the East Coast, and with a smaller budget.

1934 WORLD CUP

The 1934 World Cup was awarded to Italy, and the United States had to qualify for the finals. Oddly, FIFA decided the Americans would play Mexico in a one-game playoff slated to take place in Rome. The loser would be forced to travel back across the Atlantic Ocean after just one game; the winner would take part in the 16-team tournament. The game also marked the start of a regional rivalry with Mexico that endures to this day.

The team's 19-man roster was chosen following a series of three games. The first saw the United States take on a group of Pennsylvania League All-Stars on May 2, 1934. The United States won, 8–0, with Aldo "Buff" Donelli and Werner Nilsen scoring hat tricks. Two days later, the team lost to the ASL All-Stars, 4–0, with Stark scoring his own hat trick. The final game was played on May 5, and the United States defeated the Eastern Pennsylvania All-Stars, 2–0. Most of the players who made the final roster hailed from the strong St. Louis Soccer League, which was developing players at a rapid rate and soon became a hotbed for soccer in the United States.

On May 24, the United States, managed by Elmer Schroeder, took on Mexico at Rome's Stadio Nazionale del PNF (the Italian acronym for the ruling National Fascist Party) in front of 10,000 spectators, including dictator Benito Mussolini, flanked by black-shirted Fascist party officials. Schroeder had an exceptional soccer pedigree. He had played college soccer for the University of Pennsylvania and was coach of the Philadelphia German Americans from 1932 to 1937. With just four holdovers from the 1930 team—defenders James Gallagher and George Moorhouse, midfielder Billy Gonsalves, and striker Tom Florie—the United States was seeking to participate in its second straight World Cup.

A newcomer, however, would make all the difference that day. Donelli—nicknamed "Buff" because of his fascination with William "Buffalo Bill" Cody—scored four goals as the Americans downed Mexico, 4–2. Donelli's performance marked only the second time in team history that a player had tallied four times, equaling Archie Stark in a 6–1 win against Canada in 1925. Despite the big win, this U.S. side was considerably weaker than the one that had played at the World Cup just four years earlier. In Tony Cirino's book *U.S. Soccer vs the World*, Cirino noted, "There was no effort to get to know one another's playing styles." Donelli said training consisted of "just practicing movements up in front, like passing for forwards and crossovers from the outside men." He added,

> It is not a real big practice because there is no defense moving and you don't know where the heck to move and in those days we did not move like they do now. You played center forward, you would be a center forward. You had to make your opening from the defense as you could and you did not stray too far away from that one position.

Three days after defeating Mexico, the United States took on host Italy at Stadio Nazionale del PNF in front of 25,000 fans. Mussolini was again present. The Americans were no match for the mighty Italians, who jumped out to a 3–0 lead at halftime. The United States would go on to lose that afternoon, 7–1, with the lone goal coming from Donelli in the 57th minute. For the Americans, the World Cup was over after just one game. The *Philadelphia Inquirer* reported that after the tournament, Gonsalves said, "Losing to Italy was no disgrace. . . . We complimented ourselves in getting that one lonely goal against a team of that caliber." The Italians went on to win the tournament, much to the delight of Mussolini's propaganda machine.

ALDO "BUFF" DONELLI

Aldo Donelli was born on July 22, 1907, in Morgan, Pennsylvania, and died on August 9, 1994, in Fort Lauderdale, Florida. He played for the United States in the 1934 World Cup.

Career: Donelli began his pro career in 1925, signing with Morgan F.C. in western Pennsylvania. Between 1929 and 1938, he played for various teams, including the Curry Silver Tops in 1934. Donelli earned the nickname "Buff" because he was a fan of famous bison hunter William "Buffalo Bill" Cody. He was inducted into the U.S. National Soccer Hall of Fame in 1954. Donelli also had a successful football career in college, playing for Duquesne University as both a halfback and punter.

National Team: Although Donelli had a brief U.S. career (making only two appearances), his impact was big. He scored all four of the team's goals in a 4–2 victory against Mexico, a game that served as a one-game playoff to qualify for the 1934 World Cup. He became the first American player to score a hat trick in his first appearance—a mark equaled only by Sacha Kljestan in 2009. Donelli went on to score the only U.S. goal in a 7–1 loss to Italy in the first round of the World Cup.

Coaching: Although he never managed a soccer team, Donelli would go on to coach football at Duquesne University, Columbia University, and Boston University, as well as for the Pittsburgh Steelers and Cleveland Rams of the NFL. During the 1941 season, he coached both Duquesne and the Steelers, becoming the only man to coach a college and pro team at the same time. As the *New York Times* noted, Donelli "nailed down two singular footnotes to sports history: one as the only American to score a goal in the 1934 World Cup and the other as the only man to coach a college and National Football League team at the same time." He also served in the U.S. Navy during the latter part of World War II.

Family: Donelli retired to Florida, but he had suffered for some time from aplastic anemia, a rare disease in which the marrow ceases to produce blood cells, according to an obituary published in the student-run *Columbia Spectator* newspaper. Donelli died as a result of complications from the disease. He had a wife named Dolores, and the couple had one son, Richard, a dentist who quarterbacked the Columbia Lions and was named the school's MVP in 1958, and one daughter, Melinda.

Photo 2.2. Aldo "Buff" Donelli was one of the U.S. team's first stars. (National Soccer Hall of Fame Archive)

1936 OLYMPICS

Political propaganda was also on the mind of Adolf Hitler as Berlin prepared to host the 1936 Summer Olympics. After all, these were the same Olympic Games the Nazi's were touting as showcasing the best of the Aryan race, a myth dispelled when track and field star Jesse Owens of the United States captured four gold medals. The USFA debated whether to send a team to compete. By the time a decision was made, there was little time to raise money or prepare for the tournament. Schroeder, now USFA president, chose Francis Cavanaugh to coach the team. Cavanaugh was serving as a trainer for the Philadelphia German Americans at the time, and the U.S. roster, consisting of 17 players, was mostly made up of players from the team, winner of the U.S. Open Cup that year. The team set off for Germany, where it played two warm-up games ahead of the Olympics.

On August 3, the United States faced Italy again in the single-elimination tournament. While the Italians maintained a strong lineup, the United States kept the game close. Scoreless at halftime, the Italians took the lead in the 58th minute, with a score by Annibale Frossi. It turned out to be the game's only goal. While the Americans struggled to score, the game at Berlin's Poststadion is mostly remembered for an incident that the *Guardian* newspaper described as follows in 2011:

> The Italians, with a completely different side to the one who triumphed in the 1934 World Cup but with the same manager, Vittorio Pozzo, took on the USA and won, 1–0, thanks, in part, to an incident that may have gone some way towards establishing stereotypes that persist even now: The defender Achille Piccini clattered two American players so badly that they were unable to continue, and when the German referee made to intervene, Italian players surrounded him, covered his eyes, and held his arms by his sides as they dished out more punishment to their opponents. Incredibly, the referee was so shocked and/or intimidated that he neglected to send any Italians off before allowing play to resume.

The official box score provided by FIFA says another Italian player, Pietro Rava, was sent off in the 53rd minute by Carl Weingartner. Nonetheless, this farcical incident marred the match and led the Italians to victory. Italy would go on to add a gold medal to its trophy case by tournament's end. For the Americans, the loss would count as the only official match the team played that year.

With Europe facing the imminent threat of war and the situation growing more and more tense, the United States decided not to participate in the 1938 World Cup (where Italy repeated as champion) in France. The United States would officially enter the war in 1941, with the Japanese bombing of Pearl Harbor. As a result, the national team was inactive from 1938 to 1946. FIFA canceled the 1942 and 1946 World Cups and decided to host its next tournament in 1950, in Brazil. In 1945, the country's national soccer organization formally changed its name from the United States Football Association to the United States Soccer Football Association.

NORTH AMERICAN CUP

The United States got back on the field in 1947, participating in the North American Cup, played in Cuba. The Americans lost both matches, 5–2 to Cuba and 5–0 to Mexico, both in Havana. The U.S. team that year was made up entirely of players from the Ponta Delgada Soccer Club, based in Fall River, Massachusetts, a team formed by the local Portuguese community, which had moved there and brought the love of the sport with them. The team had become the first club to win both the National Challenge Cup and the National Amateur Cup in the same season.

With World War II over and American servicemen returning from duty, leagues like the ASL once again featured full rosters. Such players as Manuel Martin, Joe Ferreira, Ed Souza, and John Souza would participate in the 1948 Olympics in London (where the Americans would lose, 9–0, to Italy in the first round). Both Souzas, who were not related, would represent the United States in the 1950 World Cup.

3

The Big Upset: 1950–1959

By 1950, the World Cup had become a tournament more teams wanted to participate in. Thirty-four teams entered the qualification process, including the United States, for one of the final 16 spots available. The United States was placed in Group 9 of the qualifying tournament with Mexico and Cuba. With the top two teams in the group advancing to the finals, the United States had to get the best of Cuba in its two head-to-head games to move forward.

On the domestic club level, the United States featured an alphabet soup of college and regional leagues from which national team players—of all levels and ages—were developed. The lack of a cohesive vision and no national pro league meant the national team suffered. The ASL, now in its second incarnation since 1933, was small in scale and operated primarily in the Northeast. A series of regional circuits centered in several large cities fed a steady stream of talent to the national team. Some of the biggest included the St. Louis Soccer League, Chicago's National Soccer League, New York's German American Soccer League, and the Greater Los Angeles Soccer League. The game thrived at the local level. Immigrants who had brought the game with them from across the Atlantic made sure to keep it alive, but that had not been enough to propel the sport into the consciousness of the larger American culture.

1950 WORLD CUP

The qualifying tournament, which doubled as the North American Confederations Cup, was played from September 4 to September 25, in

Mexico City. The Americans, a group of semipro players coached by the Scottish-born Bill Jeffrey, would finish second, after defeating Cuba, 5–2, on September 21, at Estadío de los Deportes, in front of 60,000 fans. Two goals from Pete Matevich put the team in the World Cup. Matevich, however, would not be selected for the World Cup team and did not travel to Brazil for the finals. Jeffrey had played as a young man and went on to work as a mechanic with the Pennsylvania Railroad. He would go on to coach the company's soccer team. He was offered the coach's position at Penn State in 1925, when his team played an exhibition game against the college. He would hold that job for 27 seasons, which included a 65-game unbeaten streak that began in 1932 and stretched to 1941. He had been offered the national team job just two weeks before the start of the World Cup.

The team had been chosen by a select committee that had included federation officials. The United States did have the aid of three naturalized citizens: defender and team captain Eddie McIlvenny (Scotland), center-forward Joe Gaetjens (Haiti), and defender Joe Maca (Belgium). The roster also included the unrelated John Souza and Ed Souza. But the team also had some notable absences, including talented stars Benny McLaughlin and Jack Hynes. McLaughlin could not travel with the team because he had planned to get married, and Hynes was left off the roster after he had derided the selection process the previous year. Hynes had been part of the 1949 team that had competed in Mexico, where fans had dubbed him the "Dangerous One." In an interview with the *Staten Island Advance* in 1994, he recalled that he had sent postcards home to New York from Mexico City. In one such missive to friend Bill Graham, a sportswriter for the *Brooklyn Daily Eagle*, Hynes mentioned how bad he felt about some players who had not been invited to play. Graham turned the letter into a story. American soccer officials were upset with Hynes and, as a result, left him off the 1950 team.

The U.S. team featured players who also had to hold regular jobs to make a living. Midfielder Walter Bahr worked as a high school teacher, goalkeeper Frank Borghi drove a hearse for his family's funeral home business, and striker Frank "Pee Wee" Wallace was a postal carrier. Borghi may have been the first really talented goalkeeper to defend the U.S. goal at the international level. He had started out as a baseball player and switched to soccer. Borghi chose to play in goal because he felt he lacked the ability to play the ball with his feet. He always threw the ball—using his strong arms as a result of years as a baseball player—and even let defenders take goal kicks. A native of St. Louis, he had helped his team, the St. Louis Simkins-Ford, win the 1948 and 1950 National Challenge Cup. He was also a World War II veteran, earning a Purple Heart and Bronze Star after fighting in the Battle of the Bulge.

WALTER BAHR

Walter Bahr was born on April 1, 1927, in Philadelphia, Pennsylvania, and is the sole surviving member of the U.S. team that upset England, 1–0, at the 1950 World Cup in Brazil.

Career: Bahr, a midfielder, began playing soccer as a teenager and signed with the Philadelphia Nationals of the ASL. He helped his club win the ASL title in 1950, 1951, 1953, and 1955. In 1956, he signed with the Philadelphia-based Uhrik Truckers, winning the ASL title that year.

National Team: Bahr made 19 appearances for the United States, scoring one goal, between 1948 and 1957. He supplied the assist that allowed Joe Gaetjens to score the winning goal against England in 1950. Bahr was inducted into the National Soccer Hall of Fame, along with the entire 1950 World Cup team, in 1976.

Coaching: Bahr went into coaching after retiring as a player. He worked as a physical education teacher at Frankford High School in Philadelphia from the late 1960s to the late 1970s. He also coached the school's soccer team. Bahr coached the Philadelphia Spartans and Philadelphia Ukrainians, both of the ASL. He coached at the NCAA level for Temple and Penn State. As Penn State coach, Bahr led the team to an NCAA Tournament berth 12 times. He was named National Soccer Coaches Association of America (NSCAA) Coach of the Year in 1979. With a NCAA coaching record of 448–70–137, Bahr was elected to the NSCAA Hall of Fame in 1995.

Family: Bahr's three sons, Casey, Chris, and Matt, entered the family business and played in the North American Soccer League. Chris and Matt later played in the NFL, each winning Super Bowls as field-goal kickers. Bahr's daughter, Davies Ann, was an All-American gymnast. Walter currently resides in suburban Philadelphia.

In goal, Borghi had not been the federation's first choice. That honor had gone to Gene Olaff. A towering 6-foot-1, Olaff was the son of a Swedish seaman who had jumped ship in New York. Olaff was born in 1920, and went on to become an established goalkeeper as a teenager with the semipro Bayonne Rangers youth team and at Bayonne High School in New Jersey. In 1936, he signed to play for the ASL's New York Brookhattan. By the time the 1950 World Cup had rolled around, Olaff was a member of Brooklyn Hispano of the ASL. He had emerged as one of that

Photo 3.1. Walter Bahr was a member of the 1950 U.S. World Cup team. (Howard C. Smith/ISI Photos)

league's best goalkeepers and was best known for his trademark baseball cap and long pants. A World War II veteran who worked as a Navy diver, Olaff continued to play soccer while working for the New Jersey State Police. He earned his first—and only—cap for the United States in 1949, in a 4–0 loss to Scotland.

Olaff declined the invitation to play in the World Cup after state police officials refused to grant him his request for a leave of absence. Fearing he would lose his eligibility to retire with a pension at age 50, he never took the trip to Brazil with the team. Instead, he stayed behind, forced to follow the team's progress in the newspapers.

Placed in Group 2 in the World Cup with England, Spain, and Chile, pundits at the time expected an early trip home for the Americans. After losing to Spain, 3–1, the United States took on England on June 29, at Estadío Independencia in Belo Horizonte. England was one of the best teams in the world at the time. Nicknamed the "Kings of Europe," the English team had won 23 of its last 30 matches. The squad had defeated Italy, 4–0, and Portugal, 10–0, on the eve of the tournament. Against the Americans, the team's star, Sir Stanley Matthews, would sit out the game. He had arrived in Brazil late after taking part in a tour of English all-stars in Canada. The decision was one the English would come to regret by game's end.

Playing in front of a crowd of 10,000, the Americans and the English squared off in what would become one of the most talked-about games in World Cup history. England, wearing blue jerseys (the last time that would happen), won the coin toss and took control of the match from the opening whistle. In the opening 12 minutes, England took five shots on goal—two of them hitting the post—and another two were neutralized by Borghi. The United States was unable to move the ball out of its half of the field, as England continued to threaten Borghi's net. An England goal would never come. The game's only goal came in the 37th minute. Bahr, who anchored the midfield, took a shot from 25 yards from the England goal. As England goalkeeper Bert Williams moved to his right to block the ball, Gaetjens dove for the ball, grazing it. The glancing header was enough to change the ball's trajectory, with the ball landing in the net to Williams's left. The Americans took a lead they would never relinquish. The crowd, most of them backing the underdogs, erupted in cheers.

Even after the goal, England continued to threaten the U.S. goal. When U.S. midfielder Charles Colombo brought down Stanley Mortensen, the English players crowded around Italian referee Generoso Dattilo, pleading for a penalty kick. But the best they could get was a free kick just outside the penalty area. The ensuing kick resulted in a Jimmy Mullen header that was saved by Borghi.

Editors for several English newspapers in London questioned the wire reports following the game—some assuming it had ended 10–1 in England's favor—figuring the score was a typographical error. The result remains one of the greatest wins by an American team in any sport in international competition. But this great victory went largely unnoticed. In fact, the only American newspaper to run an article on the game was the *St. Louis Post-Dispatch*.

Said Bahr,

> It was no fluke. The English were a very good team. The odds were 500–1 that we would win. We played our hearts out that day. We were better than them that day. There are also stories about how we walked around in straw hats and smoking cigars before the game. That never happened.

Following the final whistle, Bahr said the Brazilian crowd "ran onto the field and lifted Joe [Gaetjens] on their shoulders and paraded him around the field." He added, "The crowd had really been behind us for most of the game. The English players were really good sports. They shook our hands and were respectful."

Born and raised in Haiti, Gaetjens moved to New York to study at Columbia University and worked as a part-time dishwasher. He was not a U.S. citizen at the time, but was eligible to play for the U.S. national team after he'd expressed his intention to be naturalized a U.S. citizen (something allowable under FIFA rules at the time). He would only earn three caps with the United States and go on to play one game for Haiti in 1953, during a World Cup qualifier against Mexico. He never became a U.S. citizen. Instead, Gaetjens played soccer for a few years in France and eventually moved back to his native Haiti. He disappeared in 1963, presumably murdered because his family opposed the nation's dictator, Francois Duvalier.

Despite the improbable win against England, the Americans failed to advance past the group stage following a 5–2 loss to Chile in Recife. At the end of the tournament, John Souza was the only American player selected to the World Cup All-Star Team by Brazilian sports daily *Mundo Esportivo*. He remained the only U.S. player to be named to such a team until Claudio Reyna at the 2002 World Cup. Souza had represented the United States at the 1948 Olympics and later the 1952 Olympic Games. Like Borghi, he too was a World War II veteran, after serving in the Pacific for the U.S. Navy.

In addition, the upset of England by the Americans never resonated in the United States. It did nothing to propel the sport and garnered little to no attention. It would be another 40 years before the United States played in another World Cup. "After we beat England, there wasn't much talk about the game. The newspapers didn't cover it," Bahr recalled. "My wife was the only person to meet me at the airport when I got back from Brazil."

1954 WORLD CUP QUALIFYING

Defeating England in the World Cup did little to nothing for the national team program. The team played no games in 1951, but it did make history a year later during a trip to Scotland. On April 30, the United States took on Scotland at Hampden Park in Glasgow, in front of 107,765 fans, the biggest crowd ever to witness a U.S. match. The Americans lost, 6–0, with Borghi in goal. That year also featured the Olympics, with the USSFA putting its attention on the Helsinki Games, given the attention the newspapers were giving the competition. Again, the team was composed of players who had maintained their amateur status, including John Souza and Harry Keough. Paired against Italy in the first round, the Americans were eliminated following an 8–0 defeat.

The Americans would only play one game in 1953—a rematch against England, in the teams' first meeting since the 1950 upset. On June 8, the

Photo 3.2.   Team photo of the 1950 U.S. team that defeated England. (FIFA.com)

sides lined up for a friendly match at Yankee Stadium in New York. The game had originally been scheduled for the previous evening but was postponed a day because of rain. The decision triggered head-scratching among the English journalists who had traveled to the game, and Sir Stanley Rous, secretary of the England Football Association. "We consider soccer a game to be played in all kinds of weather in England," he told the *New York Times*. "One man who is the turf controller here ruled the game could not be played. To me, it all was completely fantastic and inconceivable."

Only 7,271 fans filed into the famed venue that day, earning the dubious distinction of being the smallest crowd to ever watch England play anywhere in the world. Soccer was clearly not the spectator sport it was in England or had been just a few decades earlier in the United States. On the field, the Americans looked hapless, even though the lineup featured such 1950 World Cup vets as Bahr and Keough. In the end, England exacted revenge with a 6–3 win, with two goals and three assists from Tom Finney. The defeat was a sign of things to come for the United States. As the federation attempted to put together a team, Mexico filed a complaint against the United States, alleging they had been planning to use players who were not citizens. The United States was never sanctioned.

The inability of the United States to qualify for a World Cup became evident months before the start of the 1954 World Cup in Switzerland. The U.S. team held tryouts, and the roster that traveled to Mexico included several veterans, two of whom were Keough and Bahr. In January of that year, the Americans embarked on a mission to qualify for the finals, participating in a three-team group, along with Mexico and Haiti. The USSFA had agreed on the eve of the qualifiers that it would play all games on the road, and the Confederation of North, Central America, and Caribbean Association Football (CONCACAF) went ahead with its plan to hold the qualifying tournament in Mexico.

On January 10, the United States lost, 4–0, to Mexico in Mexico City, in front of 60,000 fans. Four days later, again in Mexico City, the Americans would lose to the Mexicans, 3–1. The Americans wanted to forfeit the remaining two games but were urged to play on by FIFA. In April, the United States would play back-to-back games in Port-au-Prince against Haiti. The Americans won both—3–2 on April 3, and 3–0 the following day—but it wasn't enough to reach the finals.

1956 MELBOURNE OLYMPICS

The United States participated in the Olympics in Melbourne, another chance for it to make a statement at a major international tournament.

Although the original plan was for the players to work out during a two-week training camp in Los Angeles before flying to Australia, the USSFA and State Department arranged for a pre-Olympic Asian tour. The Americans recorded wins against Japan, Formosa, Singapore, and the Philippines, and lost to Korea, Hong Kong, and Indonesia. The tour's success did nothing for the team once it arrived in Australia. In the single-elimination Olympic tournament, the United States was pitted against Yugoslavia. On November 28, Yugoslavia routed the United States, 9–1. The only U.S. goal came from budding striker Al Zerhusen. Yugoslavia would go on to capture silver.

1958 WORLD CUP QUALIFYING

In its bid to qualify for the 1958 World Cup in Sweden, the United States was paired off in the North American group alongside Mexico and Canada. The team was put together just days before the start of the first game on April 7, against Mexico. It featured Bahr and Keough, along with English-born defender Terry Springthorpe and striker Lloyd Monsen, who was also famous for being a baseball pitcher. In Mexico City, the Americans again experienced defeat, this time losing to the home side, 6–0, at Estadío Olimpico.

In the starting lineup that day was forward George Brown. The English-born player had soccer in his blood. The son of Jim Brown, a member of the 1930 World Cup U.S. team, the younger Brown moved back to the United States after his father completed a successful club career in England with Manchester United and Tottenham Hotspur. George played alongside his father for two years starting in 1950, with Greenport United in the Connecticut State Amateur League, which Jim had founded after returning to the United States. George went on to play with several clubs but had the most success with the New York German Hungarians of the German American Soccer League. At that time, the team featured some of the best American talent in the country, including John Souza, Walter Bahr, and Joe Maca. Jim and George Brown make up the only father–son duo to have been inducted into the National Soccer Hall of Fame. "It was sandlot stuff for sure," Brown recalled. "We never trained as a team and just showed up for games on Sundays. Most I ever made was $25 a game, plus bonuses for each goal you scored."

Brown would earn just one cap for the U.S. national team in that 6–0 loss to Mexico, played in front of 75,000 fans. Brown bemoaned the lack of organization and training the U.S. team had in those days. "The game was on a Sunday. We flew down there and arrived late on a Friday night. We trained in 100-degree weather on a Saturday, played the next day, and got hammered," he said. "To this day, I still haven't been introduced to some of the players on that team. It's really bad to lose 6–0."

The Americans hosted Mexico for the second game on April 28, in Long Beach, California, in front of 12,700 onlookers. This time, the Americans had trained in Los Angeles for three weeks prior to the match; however, that and having home-field advantage did little to favor the squad. The Mexicans won, 7–2. As had been the case four years earlier, the Americans were virtually eliminated with two games left to play. The United States recorded twin defeats against Canada—5–1 on June 22, in Toronto, and 3–2 on July 6, in St. Louis, Missouri—to round out its bleak qualifying campaign.

4

Slump into Obscurity: 1960–1969

The 1960s were a time of change. It was also a time when college and pro sports became big business. The advent of television brought games into the living rooms of millions of Americans. Soccer—although not as successful as other sports like football and baseball—attempted to capitalize on the boom. This is also when general antipathy toward the game began to fester among an ever-growing segment of the population. Sportswriters of the time, with *New York Daily News* columnist Dick Young leading the charge, called it a "game for commie pansies." Soccer was unlike any other American sport. It had no clock stoppages and no plays as in football or baseball, and was seen largely as a game played by immigrants and those not in the American mainstream. Worst of all, soccer was a low-scoring game—a trait that made it an easy target among the sport's biggest detractors.

By the end of the decade, however, the 1966 World Cup would spur growth in the game, and a dispute between two competing leagues would give birth to a national professional circuit. Although it would take another 30 years before any of it would trickle down to the national team level, soccer had entered a new era in the United States.

The decade got off to a mixed start for the United States. The team had failed to qualify for the 1960 Rome Olympics in 1959, although a bronze medal at that year's Pan American Games, played in Chicago, had been one of the most inspiring accomplishments in a decade. The Americans scored 26 goals, 10 of them coming from Al Zerhusen. Born in Brooklyn, New York, Zerhusen moved with his family to their native Germany, where he learned to play the game. He was drafted into the U.S. Army and played for the armed forces soccer team. In 1956, he was part of a group of amateurs that represented the U.S. team at the 1956 Olympics, games that did not count as full internationals. The midfielder was widely proclaimed the best hope for getting the Americans to the 1962 World Cup finals, although it didn't turn out that way.

1962 WORLD CUP QUALIFYING

Mexico would again be the biggest impediment to the United States reaching a World Cup. Placed in Group 1 with Mexico and Canada, the Americans would play their southern neighbors twice in 1960, after Canada dropped out of the competition. The two games would be the only contests the United States would play that year. On November 6, the United States managed a 3–3 draw versus Mexico in Los Angeles, overcoming a 3–0 deficit at halftime. Zerhusen, in great form that day, tallied the game-tying goal five minutes from the end. But his heroics would not be enough a week later. The Americans were eliminated on November 13, as the Mexicans defeated the U.S., 3–0, in Mexico City. History had repeated itself for the United States.

1963 PAN AMERICAN GAMES

CONCACAF, the governing body of the North American, Central American, and Caribbean region, hosted a tournament for national teams for the first time, similar to the European Championship and Copa America, the competition held to determine a South American champion. While the Americans did not participate in the inaugural event (or the other four editions held every two years through 1971, before the 1973 tournament served the dual purpose of also being the World Cup qualifying tournament), it did field a team for the Pan American Games. Held in Sao Paulo, Brazil, the Americans went 0–4 in the first round. The United States posted losses against Brazil (10–0), Argentina (8–1), Chile (10–2), and Uruguay (2–0). Outscored 30–3 in pool play, it can be considered the worst showing by a U.S. soccer team, at any level ever, at a soccer tournament. The Americans, however, had been focused on qualifying for the 1964 Olympics in Tokyo. The team included many players from St. Louis, including striker Carl Gentile. He had grown up in St. Louis and played for St. Louis University, where he would lead the team to the NCAA title in 1965. The team had also a Midwestern flavor thanks to its coach, Chicago-born George Meyer, who had coached the national team during a brief stint in 1957. He and Gentile would be reunited when Meyer took on coaching duties with the St. Louis Stars in 1971.

The qualifying tournament for the Tokyo Games, which took place in Mexico City, saw the United States lose on March 16, to Suriname, 1–0. The Americans overcame the shocking defeat two days later, beating Panama, 4–2, thanks to a Gentile hat trick. A 2–1 loss to Mexico, the region's undisputed power, in the deciding game sealed the fate of the United States. The lone American goal was scored by Gentile, who went on to attempt professional careers in baseball and football after his time playing for the St. Louis Stars. He played for the St. Louis Cardinals in their minor-league system and later tried out as a kicker for the Houston Oilers. The Americans would fail to qualify for the Olympics.

The only other game the United States would play that year was a friendly against England at New York's Downing Stadium. The May 27 matchup was organized as a pit stop for a traveling England team on its way to Rio de Janeiro to play Brazil, Argentina, and Portugal. The Americans, 13 years after the 1950 World Cup upset, were no match for England. The 5,000 fans in attendance saw a lackluster U.S. team and an English side that was riding a five-game winning streak. England took the lead after just two minutes and never looked back, winning 10–0, and recording the most lopsided victory by an English team since World War II. Roger Hunt scored four goals, as U.S. goalkeeper Uwe Schwart had no chance. For Schwart, it marked the first and only time he would play for the United States. Writing in the *New York Times*, Michael Strauss contended, "The powerful English offensive kept the ball in United States territory almost all the way. Indeed, the game's final statistics revealed that even had Gordon Banks, the victors' goalie, been sitting in a rocking chair in front of the nets, the English probably would have won."

1966 WORLD CUP QUALIFYING

The United States would play just four games in 1966—all World Cup qualifiers—in another failed effort to reach the finals, hosted by England that summer. Mexico entered as favorites to qualify. The United States, meanwhile, featured a host of new faces, including German-born striker Willy Roy. Once again, the Americans were a hastily put together bunch. With little time to train and prepare, the team looked weak but fared respectably against the region's top-tier opponents. In four games, the Americans would lose (2–0), draw (2–2) against Mexico, and record a win (2–1) and a draw (1–1) versus Honduras in the three-team round-robin tournament. The draw versus Mexico on March 7, in Los Angeles, was considered a massive achievement. The defeat five days later in Mexico City was predictable, although the Americans had scored two goals at Estadío Azteca that were disallowed, including one from Roy that looked to be legitimate.

WILLY ROY

Willy Roy was born on February 8, 1943, in Treuberg, Germany. The striker played for several National Professional Soccer League (NPSL) and National American Soccer League (NASL) teams, as well as for the United States during the late 1960s and early 1970s.

Career: Roy moved to Chicago with his family at age six. He got his start playing with semipro Chicago-area teams before turning pro with the NPSL's Chicago Spurs. In 1968, after the NPSL and the United Soccer Association merged to form the NASL, the Spurs relocated to Kansas City. Roy went with them, scoring six goals in 15 appearances during the 1968 season. In 1971, Roy signed with the St. Louis Stars, taking the team to the NASL championship game a year later, only to lose to the New York Cosmos. He closed his club career with the expansion Chicago Sting in 1975, playing in 14 games.

National Team: Roy made his U.S. debut in 1965, during a 1966 World Cup qualifier versus Mexico. He became their best player in 1968, a year in which he played in eight games, scoring six goals. In that span, the Americans went an impressive 4–3–1. During World Cup qualifying for the 1974 World Cup, Roy scored in three straight matches, giving him a U.S. record six goals in qualifying matches. The next American player to score in three consecutive matches would be Cobi Jones in 2000. Roy's record of six goals for the national team stood until 2001, when Earnie Stewart scored his seventh goal in qualifying. Roy made 20 appearances for the United States, recording 10 goals. He was inducted into the National Soccer Hall of Fame in 1989.

Coaching: After retiring, Roy became an assistant coach for the Chicago Sting in 1976. In 1979, he was promoted to head coach. In 1981, he managed the Sting to a 23–9 record, guiding them to the NASL title. In 1984, Roy coached the Sting to a second NASL title, the last time the league would crown a champion before folding. He also coached the Sting during its time as an indoor team in the Major Indoor Soccer League (MISL) from 1979 to 1986. In 1987, he was named head coach of the men's soccer team at Northern Illinois University. The school announced in 2003 that it was not renewing Roy's contract after the Huskies endured three straight losing seasons. He finished his NCAA career with a coaching record of 142–131–22, guiding the team to two conference championships.

Present Day: Roy remains involved with soccer and currently owns and operates the Willy Roy Soccer Dome, an indoor soccer facility in Chicago, and an adjacent bowling alley.

Photo 4.1. Willy Roy was one of the U.S.'s most-prolific scorers in the late 1960s. (Willy Roy Soccer Dome)

"First off, we were playing in a stadium that was jam-filled with people who were all against you," defender Bob Kehoe recalled in a 2014 interview for the *St. Louis Post-Dispatch*, adding,

> So you're trotting around, trying to get loose, trying to calm yourself down. . . . Then you looked at this field a little more closely and you thought, "Oh my God. They take this serious down here, don't they?" because the field was surrounded by a moat. And the moat was empty, so that people wouldn't jump in and try to swim across. It was about 12 or 14 feet wide and about 12 feet deep. Then you looked around some more and noticed that, surrounding you, with their backs to the field and facing the crowd, were armed soldiers. And then you thought, "Do we really want to try to win this game?"

The Americans would finish second, to Mexico, and again fail to reach the finals. Both U.S. goals against Honduras came via Scottish-born forward Ed Murphy, who would go on to become a mainstay on the team and make 18 appearances, until his last one in 1969. Even that wasn't enough for the national team to remain in a malaise. Often on the losing end of lopsided defeats, the Americans needed more than just a standout player or two to elevate the program. Murphy typified the player of the time. He spent most of his career playing in Chicago as an amateur in the city's National Soccer League. He spent only one season as a pro (with the NASL's Chicago Mustangs in 1968) and is remembered for scoring the lone goal in an 8–1 U.S. loss to England in 1959.

1970 WORLD CUP QUALIFYING

The United States was placed in Group 1 in the first round of qualifying for the World Cup finals in Brazil. The Americans had gone 3–0–1 in 1968, to finish ahead of Canada and Bermuda to reach the semifinal round. The team's success had come as a direct result of the creation of the NASL in 1968. The year before, the FIFA-sanctioned United Soccer Association (founded in 1966) and the renegade National Professional Soccer League (founded in 1967) had ended a two-year dispute and merged on December 7, 1969, to form the NASL. Although teams relied mostly on foreign talent, the new league did give American players a place to develop and grow.

With many players from Europe and South America coming to the United States to play, Americans often found it hard to break through starting lineups. The college game grew during this time, but that did little to remedy the national team's need for better, more experienced players. The NASL held a college draft, but teams at the time appeared unfamiliar with, even disinterested in, signing Americans. The United States had played just one game between 1961 and 1964, laying largely dormant. With the NASL slowly growing in popularity, the 1970 World Cup—and, more importantly, having the United States try to qualify for the tournament—was suddenly seen as a priority. But NASL teams loaded with foreigners who had defeated touring European clubs would not translate into success for the national team.

In the semifinal round, a home-and-away series against Haiti in 1969 would determine which team would reach the final, where the winner (ultimately El Salvador) would advance to the World Cup. The team's biggest obstacle, Mexico, was not there. The nation had automatically qualified as hosts. The USSFA, after selling franchise fees for the creation of pro clubs, saw its coffers fill to unprecedented levels. Dave Wangerin, in his book *Soccer in a Football World*, noted that the federation had $225,000 in its bank account and moved into an office in the Empire State Building. The federation named Phil Woosnam coach and allowed him to choose the roster. Woosnam had moved to the United States in 1966, after enjoying a successful playing career in his native England with several clubs, most notably West Ham and Aston Villa. Although hired as a coach, he played for the Atlanta Chiefs and became the team's coach in 1968. Woosnam would go on to serve as NASL commissioner from 1969 to 1983. He is credited with growing the league and securing TV contracts with ABC and CBS.

The Americans featured New York-born striker Gerry Baker, who had Scottish parents and had been on the USSFA's radar since 1966. Although he failed to play for the United States after the federation claimed it lacked the funds to pay for his airfare (he played in England with Coventry City and later Ispwich Town), that newfound money allowed them to have Baker join the rest of the team at Woosnam's request. Baker would play seven times for the United States during his career.

In World Cup qualifying, the United States lost to Haiti, 2–0, on April 20, in Port-au-Prince. In the second game on May 11, in San Diego, Haiti won again, 1–0, on a goal by Guy Saint-Vil. Baker came closest to tying the score, but his close-range attempt—the best the United States had to offer the entire game—went over the crossbar. The USSFA's reaction said it all. In a statement, the federation wrote, "We are still playing soccer in a country where the native American has little or no interest, and we are still largely dependent on ethnic groups as spectators, who, unfortunately, would rather go and see foreign teams play than their own United States team."

The Americans would be on the World Cup sidelines once again—but the U.S. national team had indeed put together its best showing in qualifying in 20 years. Few Americans had noticed the feat. More importantly, the World Cup itself was not yet a big enough sporting event that millions of Americans would follow. That reality was still decades away.

5

Soccer's Rebirth: 1970–1979

If the 1960s brought with it a pro soccer league and deep-pocketed investors, the 1970s would be a decade of even greater extravagance. Unfortunately, the U.S. national team was mostly an afterthought, as a legion of foreign superstars—most notably Brazilian star Pelé—flooded the NASL. Crowds got larger and the league grew better and more popular, but the national team did not improve. In CONCACAF, Mexico continued to dominate. The Americans, however, were still in a position where the NASL was helping to develop players. The hope continued to be that the NASL would develop them into quality national team players.

1972 MUNICH OLYMPICS

In 1971, the USSFA hit the reset button on the national team. Managed by Bob Guelker, who had coached St. Louis University to five NCAA titles (1959, 1960, 1962, 1963, and 1965) and served as USSFA president from 1967 to 1969, the United States put the 1972 Olympics in Munich in its sights. Although appearances for the Olympic team had not counted as full internationals since 1956, American players still saw prestige in qualifying for it. In fact, the United States had taken part in six Olympic soccer tournaments up to that point and had not qualified for one since the 1956 Games in Melbourne, Australia.

Guelker used college players—in keeping with the Olympic rules that only unpaid amateurs could participate in the Summer Games—to rebuild his team. This would also lay a foundation for the full national team

AL TROST

Al Trost was born on February 7, 1949, in St. Louis, Missouri. The midfielder played both in the NASL and MISL, and represented the United States throughout much of the 1970s.

Career: Trost played for St. Louis University, winning the NCAA title in 1969 and 1970. He won the Hermann Trophy both years—only one of three players to do so—as the best college player in the country. He began his pro career in 1973, playing with the St. Louis Stars of the NASL. When the franchise moved to Anaheim in 1978, to play as the California Surf, Trost remained with the team. Despite being its top scorer, the team traded Trost to the Seattle Sounders. Trost jumped the NASL ship in 1979, to play one season of indoor soccer with the MISL's New York Arrows, at the time the league's most successful franchise. In 2006, Trost was inducted into the National Soccer Hall of Fame.

National Team: Trost finished college in 1970, but he opted not to turn pro so he could play for the U.S. Olympic team. He played in eight of the team's 11 qualifying matches to reach the 1972 Munich Games. He played in two of the three United States' games at the Olympics. Trost earned his first senior national team cap in 1973. He went on to captain the U.S. team during the 1974 and 1978 World Cup qualifying. In total, he made 14 appearances for the United States, scoring one goal.

Coaching: Trost coached the St. Louis Steamers in 1981, but was fired from the MISL team in January 1983. He had coached high school soccer during his playing days. He managed McCluer North High School in Florissant, Missouri, taking them to the 1974 Missouri state championship. Most recently, Trost coached the Parkway South High School boys' and girls' teams, and he continues to be involved in the game by hosting summer soccer camps.

Family: He has a wife, Jewel.

for the remainder of the decade as college stars were signed to NASL contracts. The players called up to Olympic team duty were Hermann Trophy winner Al Trost, goalkeeper Shep Messing, and defender Casey Bahr, son of Walter Bahr. In the first round of qualifying, the United States opened with a 1–1 draw versus El Salvador on July 18, in Miami. A week later, on July 25, the Americans defeated Barbados, 3–0, in Miami. Another draw against El Salvador on the road in San Salvador, 1–1, on August 15, and a second victory versus Barbados, 3–1, on August 22, triggered a tiebreaker match to decide who would qualify for the second round.

Photo 5.1. Al Trost (left) during his NASL days. (nasljerseys.com)

Played on neutral ground in the sweltering heat of Kingston, Jamaica, in front of 4,000 onlookers, the United States and El Salvador battled to a 1–1 draw on September 18. Trost scored for the United States in the fourth minute of extra time; the Salvadorans responded with a Luis Zapata free kick in the 112th minute. With temperatures soaring to 105 degrees on field level, the outcome would be decided via a penalty shootout. Messing, who attended Harvard University, tried to psych out his opponents on El Salvador's fourth kick. Tied 3–3, Mario Castro stepped up for the kick. That's when Messing peeled off his shirt and began shouting at Castro in an attempt to strike fear into him. His shirt back on, Messing returned to his line. The bizarre move worked—Castro's kick went wide. Trost scored his kick to make it 4–3, while Luis Coreas tied it with one kick left for the United States. Horst Stemke put his shot low and to the right of goalkeeper Ricardo Martinez to put the United States through to the next round.

The second round of qualifying featured four teams—the United States, Mexico, Jamaica, and Guatemala—with two teams going through to the Olympics. The United States would finish the final round with a 5–1–1 record, qualifying for Munich, along with Mexico.

At the Olympics, the United States was placed in Group A, with host West Germany, Morocco, and Malaysia. On August 27, the Americans recorded a scoreless draw versus Morocco. Two days later, the United States lost to Malaysia, 2–0. On August 31, playing in front of 70,000 spectators at Olympic Stadium in Munich, West Germany routed the United States, 7–0. The Americans took only one point from three matches, but the experience proved invaluable.

1974 WORLD CUP QUALIFYING

While the Olympic team reached its goal, the full national team, guided by coach Bob Kehoe, aimed to rebuild in 1972, and qualify for the 1974 World Cup. The federation gave Kehoe an assistant coach, Walter Czychowycz, who was vice president of the ASL, and a budget to travel and scout players. Kehoe, a defender during his playing days, had made four appearances for the United States in 1965, where he served as team captain. He grew up surrounded by the game in St. Louis but after high school spent five years as a minor-league baseball player in the Philadelphia Phillies and St. Louis Cardinals farm systems. He went on to play pro soccer for the St. Louis Stars and, in 1969, became the first American to manage a team in the NASL when the Stars named him head coach.

The year 1972 had started off promisingly but would again end in disappointment. The player pool was largely shallow. The development of American players was still chiefly the responsibility of colleges. The decade would continue to be tough for the national team as it pertained to attaining results. Qualifying for the World Cup remained an elusive dream, while domestically Americans were becoming more and more interested in the sport, albeit to watch aging European soccer stars take the field for their favorite NASL teams.

The Americans opened qualifying on August 20, with a 3–2 road loss to Canada in St. John's, Newfoundland. The United States hosted the Canadians in Baltimore on August 29, in much need of a win. What the Americans got was a hard-fought 2–2 draw. The team's next game, on September 3, against Mexico at Mexico City's Estadío Azteca, ended in a 3–1 loss. Roy scored the only goal for the United States. Seven days later, the United States hosted Mexico in Los Angeles, needing a win. But Mexico again proved too difficult, and the match ended 2–1 for the visitors. Mexico would go on to reach the finals by virtue of its win versus Canada, eliminating the United States.

1978 WORLD CUP QUALIFYING

There was a seismic shift in the popularity of the game in the mid-1970s. In 1974, the country's national soccer association dropped the word "football" from its name and became known as the United States Soccer Federation. The USSF hired its first full-time coach, naming Dettmar Cramer to the position. Cramer, who had conducted soccer clinics in the United States and worked with youth teams in the past, boasted an outstanding resume. He'd coached West Germany in the 1954 World Cup and Japan's Olympic team. Cramer knew he had a tough task ahead of him if the United States was to reach the 1978 World Cup finals in Argentina. He knew the only way the Americans could qualify was for the coach to scout and choose the players, tapping into the burgeoning NASL for talent. In the early 1970s, Cramer had brought professionalism to the USSF. He helped create a national coaching school and a curriculum that would help a future generation of American coaches.

The NASL had become a powerhouse. The New York Cosmos, bankrolled by Warner Communications, made the biggest statement of them all in 1975, by signing Pelé, a three-time World Cup champion and, by the end of the decade, a household name in the United States, alongside other sports icons of the time. Considered the best player of all time, the Brazilian had spent his entire career with one club, Santos of Brazil, and had declined offers from European clubs for years. Pelé's two years with the Cosmos would forever change the sport in the United States. Although the NASL saw a growth in attendance and garnered mainstream popularity, albeit for a brief time, the league would eventually disappear in a sea of red ink. But Pelé's arrival inspired a generation of children to play the game for years to come—something that would impact the future of the national team in a way bigger than the arrival of a new coach.

Cramer would only coach the United States for two games during a period of five months, leaving in January 1975, to manage German club Bayern Munich. Cramer had been brought on for a four-year deal, but the German decided to break the verbal contract in favor of returning to Germany. As a result, Al Miller, who had coached the NASL's Philadelphia Atoms, replaced him on an interim basis. Manny Schellscheidt, who coached the Rhode Island Oceaneers to the 1974 ASL championship, took over for Miller later that year. None had been able to achieve any real success with the team.

While the still-nascent NASL prospered, the U.S. national team struggled to get its footing. When the league decided to create and host the Bicentennial Cup—a tournament aimed at celebrating the country's 200th anniversary—it invited Italy, England, and Brazil to compete against

Team America, a selection of NASL all-stars. Its objective was to promote the fledgling league, not the national team. While Team America, which featured such international stars as Pelé, Bobby Moore, and George Best in the lineup, would lose all three of its matches (versus Italy, England, and Brazil), it was no sign of what the national team could do. Brazil would win the round-robin tournament that summer. The team had only featured four Americans—goalkeepers Arnie Mausser and Bob Rigby, as well as defenders Peter Chandler and Bobby Smith. Julie Veee, who was born in Hungary, later became a naturalized U.S. citizen. It was further proof that the NASL was more interested in putting on a great show than building and improving the national team's fortunes.

In 1976, the USSF hired Czychowycz, a one-time U.S. assistant coach. He was given the task of trying to help the team qualify for the World Cup. The Americans found themselves in a surprising position after drawing Mexico, 0–0, on October 3, in Los Angeles, and defeating Canada, 2–0, on October 20, in Seattle. With the United States and Canada level on points, with five each, and behind Mexico in the first round of qualifying, a tiebreaker match needed to be played. Czychowycz's team, which featured Mausser in goal and Veee as a striker, had exceeded expectations. Mausser was the finest goalkeeper the United States had produced since Frank Borghi. Famous for throwing with his right hand and kicking with the left, Mausser grew up in Brooklyn, loving basketball because of his height but later deciding to use that 6-foot-5 frame to play goalie. He played for several NASL teams but is most remembered for his time as a member of the Fort Lauderdale Strikers. Veee, on the other hand, became a U.S. citizen after signing with the NASL's Los Angeles Aztecs in 1975. He had defected from the country's brutal Communist regime as a teen, opting to pursue a pro soccer career in France before joining the NASL.

The United States traveled to a neutral site, in Port-au-Prince, Haiti, on December 22, for its playoff match against Canada. The Americans had been granted two months from the end of qualifying in October to prepare for the match. The USSF wisely decided to fly the team to Port-au-Prince to train, as well as play a series of friendlies against Haiti. The sides played three times that November, all ending in scoreless draws. The Americans would suffer a blow when Al Trost, its strongest offensive weapon, fell ill on the eve of the game with a stomach virus. Trost played nonetheless but proved to be a nonfactor. It would be his last competitive game for the United States. He would go on to play four more friendlies before ending his national team career.

In a 2015 interview with USSoccer.com, Trost recalled that Czychowycz was able to get the federation to invest the money and logistics to put the Americans in a position to qualify for the World Cup:

Walt did a great job of preparing us for these games. Before this [qualify-ing] tournament, I don't think the federation really put the money or effort in to set a stage for American players to be challenged and develop for in-ternational soccer. In the past, we got together 24 hours before a game and that was it. Walt did a good job of convincing the federation into getting us into Denver, training at high altitude ahead of games [to face Mexico], and I thought he prepared us well.

In the end, none of that mattered against Canada. The United States went down early, with Canada taking the lead after 21 minutes off a goal from Vancouver Whitecaps striker Brian Budd. The Americans, in desper-ate search of an equalizer, pushed forward. Defender Bob Lenarduzzi doubled the score for Canada 10 minutes from time. Lenarduzzi's rocket of a shot beat Mausser, ending the U.S. hopes for a World Cup appearance. Robert Bolitho scored a third goal in the 87th minute to give Canada a 3–0 victory. If anything, the NASL had helped Canada reach the next round of World Cup qualifying. The Americans were out of luck once again.

6

On the Verge of Success: 1980–1988

The 1980s were a time of great reflection and transformation for the national team program and the game as a whole in the United States. The first half of the decade saw the NASL's demise, ushering in a barren time for soccer in the country. Soccer, it appeared, had been merely a fad for most sports fans throughout the United States. Pelé's legacy had run its course. Growing in popularity was an indoor version of the sport, played in basketball arenas on hockey rink-sized fields in midsized markets. It was an easy game to market to families looking for something to do during the winter months, especially for those who enjoyed a high-scoring product. Pelé had given way to a group of such new foreign-born stars as Steve Zungul, Preki, and Tatu.

Before the NASL folded, it continued its lack of cooperation with the U.S. national team. The NASL was about selling the sport to the American sports public at large, not ensuring that the United States could compete on a global level with other countries. The early 1980s marked an escalation in the war between the league and the national team. The NASL, unlike most leagues in the world, was not required to release its players for national team duty for official FIFA-sanctioned matches; therefore, the Americans were often forced to field college players to round out the roster. Any progress Walter Czychowycz had made in the late 1970s had eroded. The United States still could not compete with the best teams in CONCACAF (namely Mexico), and the NASL's continued stronghold on the domestic game did nothing to make it easier for a national team still trying to qualify for the World Cup.

What made qualifying even more difficult was the lack of a pro league where players could gain experience. In its place, players were forced to play for the MISL. The MISL began in 1978, lasting until its demise in 1992, when it was known as the Major Soccer League. The league had dropped the word *indoor* in an effort to position itself as an outdoor league after the United States was granted hosting rights by FIFA for the 1994 World Cup. The league largely functioned as the country's only professional circuit during the late 1980s and early 90s. During its 14 years of existence, teams would be based in 27 different cities. The San Diego Sockers would go on to be the league's most successful franchise, winning eight titles. Like the NASL, the league was immensely popular, particularly in medium-sized markets like Houston, Dallas, Baltimore, St. Louis, and Kansas City. While attendance grew, the league suffered many financial setbacks.

Indoor soccer was appealing to a large segment of Americans, particularly in the suburbs. It was fan friendly and affordable, and started many of the gimmicks we are used to seeing in sports today. Players would emerge from the tunnel as fake fog was piped in with the help of dry ice. Loud music would be played during most of the games, and fireworks were used to drum up excitement. It featured end-to-end action like hockey and basketball, as well as high-scoring games. It was played inside arenas during the winter months and was not beholden to the elements. The concept was so popular that it inspired the creation of the Arena Football League, a NFL-style game played on a smaller field. The league exists to this day.

The New York Arrows, who won the league's first four championships, featured Shep Messing in goal. A veteran of the Cosmos and the U.S. Olympic team, Messing typified the American player who kept playing despite the NASL's collapse. "Playing the position outdoors required 90 minutes of concentration and eight or nine moments of action. Indoors required 60 minutes of nonstop action and facing 30 or 40 shots, caroms, collisions, and fast breaks," said Messing. "Goalkeepers want action, and indoor soccer gave you that."

Despite what many considered a bastardization of the outdoor game, the MISL kept American players employed. What it did not, and could not, do was create a system that would keep players fit and prepared for the outdoor game and the task of trying to field a competitive national team that could qualify for a World Cup.

The other move to get a professional national league took place in 1990. Two regional leagues at the time—another incarnation of the American Soccer League that began in 1988, and the Western Soccer Alliance (WSA), which started in 1985—agreed to merge. The ASL's Clive Toye, the man who had helped the Cosmos sign Pelé more than a decade earlier, and the WSA's Bill Sage came together for the good of the game. Although the leagues had announced a merger in April 1989, they still operated independently and ran separate schedules, with the ASL operating as the East Conference and the renamed Western Soccer League as the West. The winners of each league would play one another for the newly formed American Professional Soccer League (APSL) title. The partnership was reminiscent of the early days of the Super Bowl—which helped propel football into the spectator sport it is today—when two separate leagues would join to prove which was best. In a 1989 press release, Toye and Sage, in a joint statement, said the merger was part of a plan to help in the "promotion of the game, the development of the American player, and the wise management of big-league soccer." Those are the same buzzwords used today when someone wants to make grandiose statements about the future of the game.

At the time, the goal of the merger was to become U.S. Soccer's sanctioned first-division league, something the federation was working on as a FIFA prerequisite to hosting the 1994 World Cup. The APSL, however, was anything but big-league soccer, although it featured such storied franchises as the Fort Lauderdale Strikers and Tampa Bay Rowdies. It also had many new franchises, notably the San Francisco Bay Blackhawks, bankrolled by deep-pocketed real estate lawyer Dan Van Voorhis.

Photo 6.1.   The U.S. team poses for a photo in 1981 during World Cup qualifying. (National Soccer Hall of Fame Archive)

Despite modest attendance figures of only a few thousand per game, the league was looking to become the country's Division I circuit, after the 1994 World Cup. Like the MISL, the APSL was not granted Division I status by U.S. Soccer, which ushered in the creation of Major League Soccer. The APSL changed its name to the A-League in 1995 and was later absorbed by the then-emerging United States Interregional Soccer League (USISL), the precursor to the United Soccer Leagues, when it finally ceased operation in 1996.

1982 WORLD CUP QUALIFYING

The road to the 1982 World Cup, which was to be held in Spain, began in 1980. The United States was placed in the Northern Zone for the first round, with Canada and Mexico. The key match for the United States came on November 11, 1980, when the Americans traveled to Mexico City. A loss would virtually eliminate the team. The 90,000 fans that packed the Estadío Azteca that afternoon would not make it easy. Neither would Mexico's lineup, which included striker Hugo Sanchez.

Sanchez was Mexico's best player during this time. A prolific scorer, he combined speed and skill to make Mexico a stronger squad. He would go on to much success a few years later with Spanish giant Real Madrid. Sanchez was known to American fans for his yearlong stint with the Sockers in 1979, when the team played in the NASL. The Americans responded with midfielder Rick Davis, a budding U.S. player and member of the New York Cosmos, playing at center back. Midfielder Perry Van der Beck, meanwhile, carried the team's offensive hopes. Van der Beck, a lethal striker in his day who was able to get past defenders with his crafty dribbling skills, would go on to be a regular in the U.S. lineup during the team's failed attempts at qualifying for the World Cup throughout the 1980s.

The Mexicans piled on the goals that day as goalkeeper Winston DuBose tried in vain to keep the loss respectable. DuBose would spend eight seasons in the NASL and go on to make 14 appearances for the national team. Despite his skill and experience, Mexico defeated the United States, 5–1, one of the most lopsided results ever recorded between the two nations.

With the Americans out, the return match against Mexico, to be played in Fort Lauderdale, Florida, two weeks later, on November 23, was nothing more than a formality. Nevertheless, the Americans did something extraordinary that day in defeating their regional rivals for the first time since 1934. Two goals from Steve Moyers, a NASL star with the Cosmos and one of five players from the New York team in the starting lineup that day, clinched the win at Lockhart Stadium. Moyers's first goal, a header,

RICK DAVIS

Rick Davis was born on November 24, 1958, in Denver, Colorado, but grew up in Claremont, California. He is widely considered the best American-born player during the NASL era. He also captained the U.S. national team throughout most of the 1980s.

Career: Davis got his start playing in the American Youth Soccer Organization (AYSO) before going on to become an All-American high school player at Damien High School in La Verne, California. In 1977, he played one season of college soccer at Santa Clara before opting to go pro. Davis went on to become one of the few Americans on a New York Cosmos team loaded with international superstars. He helped the team win three NASL titles (1978, 1980, and 1982) and was named NASL Player of the Year in 1979. In 1983, as the NASL was on the brink of folding, Davis signed with the MISL's St. Louis Steamers. He left to join the New York Express, an expansion team that featured former Cosmos players, and played for them until the team folded midway through the 1986–1987 season. In March 1987, Davis signed with the Tacoma Stars. In January 1989, he injured his knee, which led to a series of surgeries. He retired in 1990, as a member of the Seattle Storm of the Western Soccer Alliance.

National Team: Davis played for the United States from 1977 to 1988, amassing 36 appearances and seven goals. He got his start with the Olympic and Under-20 teams before being called up to the senior side. He earned his first cap on September 15, 1977, at the age of 17, against El Salvador. He also scored his first U.S. goal in that game. Davis played for the Olympic team in the 1984 Los Angeles Games, scoring two goals. That same year, he was winner of the first-ever U.S. Soccer Athlete of the Year award. In 1988, he was named captain of the U.S. national team, but knee injuries kept him sidelined. Although he tried a comeback, U.S. coach Bob Gansler never recalled him to the team, which went on to qualify for the 1990 World Cup. Davis was elected to the National Soccer Hall of Fame in 2001.

Coaching: After retiring, Davis coached the Los Angeles Salsa of the APSL. In 2004, he was named the AYSO's director of programs and, two years later, its national executive director. He left the position in May 2010.

Family: He lives with his wife in Ellsworth, Kansas, where he runs Ellsworth Steakhouse.

Photo 6.2. Rick Davis was one of the few Americans to star for the New York Cosmos. (New York Cosmos)

came off a free kick at the edge of the penalty box after 31 minutes. With the game tied, 1–1, Moyers scored the winning goal in the 65th minute, his right-footed blast catching the Mexican defense by surprise. For Moyers, it would be the only two goals he would ever score in a U.S. jersey.

A 46-year-old record had been shattered. Unfortunately, the game was not televised in the United States. It was broadcast in Mexico by Televisa, but the video remains locked in their vault. Requests to screen it—including one made during the writing of this book—were denied. It was known as the "lost tape" game until November 2016, when footage from it was revealed for the first time on Miami-based Spanish-language network Univision. It was this win that reignited the rivalry with Mexico.

However, the victory was not taken well by some in American soccer circles, including the NASL. David Litterer, writing for the American Soccer History Archives website, reported,

> The day after that game, the first U.S. victory over Mexico in World Cup competition since 1934, the Cosmos' president, Ahmet Ertegun, and captain Giorgio Chinaglia called for the resignation or firing of Czychowycz. They complained that he hadn't included more Cosmos players on the team and would not collaborate with Cosmos coach Hennes Weisweller and Rinus Michaels of the [Los Angeles] Aztecs. For now, Czychowycz refused to obey this "request" and continued to coach for one more season. However, 1981 was an inactive year for the senior team, and [Czychowycz] devoted his efforts to developing the [U.S.] youth team.

Photo 6.3.   President Ronald Reagan meets with Team America ahead of the 1984 NASL season. (The White House)

Czychowycz would be replaced in 1982, when the USSF named Karl-Heinz Heddergott director of coaching. Heddergott had managed Egypt from 1980 to 1982, with extensive connections in the German soccer federation. While Heddergott was the foreigner the USSF thought would change things, he would not. At the same time, the USSF began to promote the United States as a potential site for the 1986 World Cup, as a replacement for Colombia, which had been forced to withdraw for financial reasons. With the Summer Olympics being hosted by Los Angeles in 1984, the United States was eager to show off its stadiums and infrastructure. Although FIFA would ultimately award the World Cup to Mexico, the United States would get another chance in 1988.

1986 WORLD CUP QUALIFYING

In 1983, the USSF dusted off an idea it had initially proposed in 1976: the creation of a full-time squad of Americans that could compete on a weekly basis. The concept, known as Team America, was aimed at making the national team into a NASL franchise, with the purpose of drawing fans and getting the team ready ahead of the World Cup. It drew the USSF and NASL closer together than ever, but in the end it would prove to be a failed experiment. The NASL's attendance was dropping. Howard Samuels, the NASL's president and CEO, inherited Team America from outgoing commissioner Phil Woosnam. The USSF was more than happy to comply with the plan.

Many Americans had found it difficult to get playing time on teams stacked with foreign stars, and Team America was meant to remedy that situation. The team was coached by Alketas "Alkis" Panagoulias, who had coached his native Greece in the 1970s and the New York-based amateur club Greek American Atlas. The team would be based in Washington, D.C., and play its home games at RFK Stadium. The problem was that Samuels had no clue how to promote and market such a franchise. While players like Perry Van der Beck chose to sign with the newly formed franchise, others like Davis and DuBose opted out. Moyers, regarded as the most promising American striker at the time, instead signed with the Cosmos. Team America would go on to be a massive failure. The team—a combination of young, old, and whoever was available with a U.S. passport—finished the 1983 season with a 10–20 record, losing 15 of its last 17 matches. The squad was disbanded after one season. Washington would be without a pro soccer franchise for another decade.

Since 1954, the United States had posted a qualifying record of 8–18–7. The team, however, was trying to shake off its past problems. Panagoulias's vision was to look forward and focus on the positives. For a short period of time, it seemed to work. Panagoulias loved his adopted country and the national team, something he made clear to Samuels and the NASL. "I was almost crying when I talked about the national team," he told the *New York Times* in 2006. "They looked at me like I was crazy."

The mid-1980s also saw the team accomplish something big. Eddie Hawkins, a midfielder, came on as a sub against Ecuador on December 2, 1984. The game, part of the Miami Cup, ended in a 2–2 draw. But there was much more than the score to celebrate. Hawkins became the first African American player to appear for the national team. Although players of color had donned the U.S. jersey in the past, Hawkins had broken new ground. He would forever be soccer's version of Jackie Robinson, who had broken baseball's color barrier as a member of the Brooklyn Dodgers in 1947. It had been shameful for a team that had featured foreign-born players and naturalized citizens to have never had a native-born black appear in a match. As had been the case with many national team milestones in the past, the event went largely unnoticed. For Hawkins, it would be his only appearance for the national team. In an interview with FIFA.com in 2011, he recalled the moment:

> There were a few other black players that had been nationalized, but I did know a couple of years later that I was the first American-born (black player). There really was not much attention given to the fact that I was black and playing in the team because I knew most of the other players from

the camps. I had built those relationships through soccer, so it didn't seem strange. The good part about it being ignored was that it gave me the sense that it was my ability that got me to that level, versus any kind of favoritism. The bad part is that because nobody did a lot about it, there was no messaging like there would be today. Maybe it didn't touch as many players as it could have, which might have led them to think, "Hey, I can do that, too."

The Americans participated in the 1985 CONCACAF Championship, which doubled as the region's qualifying tournament. The Americans were placed in Group 3, with Costa Rica and Trinidad and Tobago. They would need to win the round-robin group to reach the second round. The United States opened with a 2–1 victory in St. Louis against Trinidad and Tobago on May 15. Four days later, in Torrance, California, the Americans defeated Trinidad and Tobago, 1–0, on a goal from Paul Caligiuri. What remained on the schedule were two matches—at home and away—against Costa Rica, the favorite to advance.

Optimism reigned supreme. For all the hiccups between the USSF and NASL, Panagoulias knew the player pool he had at his disposal. The cigar-chomping, no-nonsense coach had managed the senior national team and Team America, and overseen the development of the team that went 1–1–1 at the Los Angeles Olympics, and he was also instrumental in the formation of several youth teams. In a 1983 *Sports Illustrated* interview, Panagoulias oozed positivity. "This isn't some underdeveloped, underprivileged country. Even now as we talk, somewhere—in Harlem, in Tampa, in L.A., I don't know where—there are Pelés growing up," he said. "There was no compulsion for me to leave a comfortable career in Greece and come here. But I believe that American soccer has a tremendous potential for success."

The potential was there, the results were not. The two games against Costa Rica would represent another low point in a decade where there were many for the American game. The Americans were able to draw Costa Rica, 1–1, on the road on May 26, with John Kerr Jr. tallying the key goal just before halftime. The United States needed just a draw a week later at home to advance to the final round. What awaited the team at Murdock Stadium in Torrance should have been no surprise to the USSF or the players. A pro-Costa Rica crowd awaited Panagoulias's men on May 31. The USSF had, in part, scheduled the match there to maximize attendance. Home-field advantage took a back seat to ticket sales and revenue in those days.

Panagoulias relied on the formation that had gotten his team this far. Veteran Arnie Mausser tended goal, while Michael Windischmann and Kevin Crow anchored the defense. Davis and Caligiuri patrolled the midfield, tracking back to aid the backline in case the Americans were

Photo 6.4. Goalkeeper Arnie Mausser (standing, in Rowdies jersey) was the U.S.'s starting goalkeeper for much of the 1980s. (nasljerseys.com)

put on their heels early. Hugo Perez, the team's creative catalyst, joined Kerr in attack. Panagoulias's mix of NASL players and college stars kept pace with Costa Rica until the 35th minute, when a Jorge Chavez free kick outside the penalty area turned into an attempt Mausser was unable to clear. The ball found its way back into the box. Evaristo Coronado, considered one of the best Costa Rican strikers of the time, kicked it into the net. Mausser said that moment remains his biggest regret:

> I came out of my goal to punch the ball away but did not clear the ball very well, and Costa Rica scored. We had chances to score during the normal play of the game but came away empty. I believe that was the last appearance for me with the U.S. national team. To leave on such a sour note bothers me even to this day.

The United States was unable to respond effectively. They played frantically, using the flanks to try and get the ball to Kerr. It didn't work. The closest the Americans would come was in the 73rd minute, when defender Dan Canter's free kick hit the side-netting, briefly giving the illusion of a goal. Referee John Meachin of Canada even whistled it as a goal. Davis quickly scooped up the ball to place it in the midfield circle, as if to maintain the illusion it had been a legitimate goal. It wasn't until the referee's assistant—surrounded by a crowd of angry Costa Rican players—signaled to the referee that it was no goal. Canter had played for Panagoulias during the Team America experiment, missing his chance to make the Olympic team following an injury. He signed with the Cosmos after Team America folded, becoming a regular in the U.S. lineup during qualification.

As for the game, the Americans knew a draw would get them to the World Cup. But the goal never came, and Costa Rica won, 1–0. The Americans had been eliminated. Arnie Mausser, Dan Canter, Perry Van der Beck, and Angelo DiBernardo, who had come on as a sub, would never again play for the national team. Another generation of American players would miss out on the World Cup. Despite the bleak outcome, brighter days lay ahead for the national team and the beleaguered, financially strapped USSF. Davis, the best American player of his generation, would go on to play for the national team but never play in a World Cup. "I would have liked to have once played at a World Cup," Davis said, "but it just didn't work out that way."

While Mexico hosted the 1986 World Cup, the United States tried to rebuild its program. The team played only two games in 1986; however, they both proved pivotal. The side endured a massive makeover at the hands of its new coach, German-born Lothar Osiander, who took over for Panagoulias, who had amassed an unimpressive 6–7–5 record in two years. Osiander had moved to the United States with his family in 1958, and played for the University of San Francisco. He went on to coach a number of teams, including, years later, in Major League Soccer, the Los Angeles Galaxy and San Jose Clash. With Osiander at the helm, the United States rebuilt its program around college players. This was out of necessity. With the MISL refusing to release players for international duty, Osiander was left with few options and turned to the NCAA ranks for talent.

The team assembled in February of that year for the Miami Cup, a six-team exhibition tournament staged entirely at the storied, 75,500-seat Orange Bowl. The field featured the host, the United States, as well as Uruguay, Canada, Jamaica, Paraguay, and Colombian club Deportivo Cali. The United States joined Uruguay and Canada in the "Sunshine Division," while the other three teams were placed in the "Citrus Division." The tournament had a baseball spring training feel to it. For the United States, however, it was a chance to test the team against two fairly competitive squads.

Uruguay and Canada both qualified for the 1986 World Cup, so the U.S. national team was facing two teams that were preparing for Mexico. Uruguay, in particular, was on an upswing. They would reach the knockout round of the 1986 World Cup and win the 1987 Copa America. The United States played Canada on February 2, in front of a small crowd of 5,182 in a cavernous football stadium. They fielded a lineup that years later would make the nation proud. David Vanole was in goal, with Paul

Krumpe and Jimmy Banks (Mike Windischmann would replace him in the second half), along with Brent Goulet, spearheading the attack. The result was a scoreless draw.

"This was my first invite to the national team," recalled Krumpe. "I was 23 and had recently just graduated from UCLA. . . . We had a very good group of college guys, but we needed to gain some valuable experience with these international tournaments. This proved to be very valuable experience indeed." Krumpe said Osiander "made us work and found a way to allow us to enjoy ourselves at the same time. Not an easy thing to do, especially at this level." He added, "I felt I knew what he wanted from me, individually, and for the team as a whole."

Goulet was a promising player at the time. Named U.S. Soccer Player of the Year in 1987, he played for FC Portland in the Western Soccer Alliance and led the league in scoring, with nine goals, during the 1986 season. His scoring caught the attention of the national team, and he later played for the U.S. Olympic team. Goulet only made eight appearances for the senior U.S. squad. He went on to a successful career in Germany's lower division but disappeared from the radar screen. He retired in 2001.

Another member of the team, Bruce Murray, had more staying power. He had recollections similar to those of Krumpe when it came to that 1987 camp, calling Osiander's style "pretty strict" but also referring to him as a man who could "have a laugh with the group." Murray also said Osiander called him Murphy, which drove him crazy. He said, "I'd tell him it was Murray, and he'd say, 'Okay, Murph.'"

In many ways, Murray would go on to be the heart and soul of this U.S. team in the years that followed. In 1993, at the time of his retirement, his 21 goals in 85 games for the team made him the squad's all-time leading scorer. He played college soccer with Clemson but became a pro in the post-NASL years. He would go on to play full-time with the national team. Known for his bursts of energy and ability to score with both his head and his powerful feet, Murray was both a striker and a midfielder.

In their second match, on February 7, the United States took on Uruguay in front of 15,852 spectators, needing a win to advance to the final. Uruguay, 3–1 winners against Canada, needed just a draw. Osiander changed things up a bit, starting Murray in midfield. Uruguay (who would go on to win the Miami Cup) was without its star, Enzo Francescoli, but the country did field a team of mostly regulars. Against the two-time world champions, the United States took the lead with Murray in the ninth minute. "I was a right-sided midfielder tasked with playing simple and not trying to do much," Murray recalled. "Anyway, I intercepted a pass in our half. I looked to find someone to pass to but was immediately under pressure, so I had to beat two players off the dribble. Now I'm 35 yards out. Still no help—so took another touch and let it fly."

The ball, like a "rocket," Murray recalled, sailed into the upper left corner out of the reach of goalkeeper Fernando Alvez. "One of the best strikes of my life," said Murray. The Americans tried in vain to extend the lead, but it was Uruguay who would find the back of the net, tying the score with a goal from Carlos Aguilera 15 minutes from the end. Although the United States had failed to advance to the final, two draws from two games were considered a success for a young team that had never played together before. Krumpe, who went on to play indoor soccer with the Chicago Sting, recalled that using college players turned out to be the right call, saying,

It was a huge transition to play indoor soccer full time and then quickly become an international outdoor player. I had an excellent fitness base as a high school distance runner, a college defender who liked to join the attack and was easier to make the transition than most guys. It was not easy.

7

Shot Heard 'Round the World: 1989–1999

The 1990s would be a decade punctuated by success, World Cup appearances, and the creation of a new pro league. Indeed, this was an age of unprecedented growth, sowing the seeds of what the national team is today. Three things took place that set in motion the growth of the U.S. national team: the awarding of the 1994 World Cup to the United States in 1988, the national team qualifying for the 1990 World Cup a year later, and the forming of Major League Soccer (MLS) in 1996. These developments proved essential, as the game enjoyed newfound popularity in an ever-crowded American sports and entertainment landscape.

"I feel this group in 1990 was at the start of a burgeoning mushroom of soccer players in America," said Paul Krumpe, a member of the team that qualified for the World Cup. He added,

> I had only played for one coach prior to college who had played the game of soccer before, and I think that was true of most of the U.S. players at that time. Now, there are very few players who reach a Division I college program who have not played club soccer and even high school soccer for years for coaches who have played the game at a very high level. It was simply a matter of time before the United States exploded on the international scene. MLS has certainly been the main catalyst in that regard.

Soccer was no longer a niche game enjoyed by immigrants or regionally as a recreational game. It was a sport that quickly became popular among children of all ages—giving rise to the voting bloc of suburban women in the 1992 presidential elections known as "soccer moms"—and spurred the movement of American players abroad to play for European clubs.

The biggest victory for the United States came, fittingly, on July 4, 1988, when FIFA awarded it the rights to host the 1994 World Cup. It was a moment that would forever change the course of the game in the country and led to an unprecedented growth in the sport, rivaling even that of the NASL in the mid-1970s. A 15-month campaign on the part of the USSF, led by President Werner Fricker, culminated with that historic Independence Day vote at FIFA's headquarters in Zurich, Switzerland. The U.S. bid also included a videotape message from President Ronald Reagan. By the time the executive committee cast their ballots, the United States had received 10 votes, Morocco 7, and Brazil 2. The United States had made history without kicking a ball.

At that point in time, the United States had only qualified for three World Cups (1930, 1934, and 1950) and was in the midst of trying to reach the 1990 finals in Italy, a feat it would achieve 14 months after FIFA's vote. FIFA had taken notice of the 1984 Summer Olympics. The Olympic soccer tournament, held at the Rose Bowl in Pasadena, had been a rousing success. A crowd of 101,799 had attended the final. France defeated Brazil, 2–0, for the gold medal, and FIFA officials were watching—and smiling. The stock of the United States as an organizer, particularly of a soccer tournament, grew instantly. The marketing opportunities seemed endless. FIFA not only knew that playing the World Cup in the United States would help grow the game in a country where soccer was a nonfactor, but also saw the potential windfall sponsorship dollars would bring in.

Since 1962, the World Cup had alternated between the Americas and Europe. Although Brazil had a rich history of soccer and Africa remained a continent that had never hosted a World Cup, the United States—with its government support, NFL stadiums, and great infrastructure—remained an untapped market. Indeed, the U.S. ability to market the game and lure advertisers would be a model FIFA would use for years to come. "The United States is the only unconquered continent in the soccer set," Peter Pullen, a member of the Brazilian bid delegation, told the *New York Times* following the decision. "There is a great potential for economic power, and a lot of people can make a lot of money if the games take off."

The original date of the vote had been set for June 30, but a change to July 4 gave a strong—and hopeful—hint that the United States would get the 1994 tournament. At 1:21 p.m. local time at the Movenpick Hotel, FIFA announced that the United States would host the 1994 World Cup. The American delegation celebrated. The decision was front-page news in newspapers throughout the world.

The Americans had set their sights on playing host for the World Cup years earlier. After Colombia had dropped out as host of the 1986 World Cup, the United States—with the NASL in its dying days—hastily put together a 92-page bid book, flimsy for even 1980s standards, with color photos of the proposed stadiums and little substance. In 1983, the 27-member executive committee had named Mexico as host, the first time a nation would get to host a second World Cup, after the one in 1970. For the 1994 World Cup, the USSF made a serious bid. The federation put together a 381-page bid book that cost $500,000 to produce. The book listed 18 potential venues, although only five from that book would host games: RFK Stadium (Washington, D.C.), Soldier Field (Chicago), the Cotton Bowl (Dallas), the Rose Bowl (Pasadena), and the Citrus Bowl (Orlando).

1990 WORLD CUP QUALIFYING

From boardroom success to success on the field, the USSF was determined to qualify for the 1990 World Cup finals in Italy. The Americans caught a break when FIFA disqualified Mexico from taking part after fielding overage players at youth tournaments. One of the biggest obstacles for the United States would not be there this time around. Instead, the Americans would have to tangle with other up-and-coming regional powers, like Costa Rica and Trinidad and Tobago. "The [U.S.] federation was very amateurish at that time and had no money," said Arnie Mausser. "It wasn't until the 1990s that things began to change and the federation became more professional. The team got better, the players started making more money, and more fans started showing up to home games."

The 1989 CONCACAF Championship would be the last time it would double as a World Cup qualifying tournament. In 1991, CONCACAF would host the Gold Cup, a separate regional championship that would take place in the United States every two years. For the United States, the road to Italy began on April 16, 1989, with a 1–0 loss to Costa Rica; however, victories at home versus Costa Rica (1–0) and Guatemala (2–1), as well as a key road victory (1–0 versus El Salvador on a Hugo Perez goal), put the team in position to reach the World Cup on the final day of qualifying. Although it was a team effort, it was Paul Caligiuri, a defensive midfielder and a leftover from the ill-fated 1985 team that had failed to qualify, and his lone goal against Trinidad and Tobago that gave the United States the win, officially stamping its passport to Italia 1990. The goal, later dubbed the "Shot Heard 'Round the World," may be the most famous strike in American soccer history.

Caligiuri grew up in Westminster, California, a suburb of Los Angeles, and attended UCLA. He played at the school for four years and captained the team to the NCAA title in his junior year. He went on to play for the San Diego Nomads of the Western Soccer Alliance, a regional league, and featured in a 1986 FIFA All-Star Game. It was there where his play in midfield attracted the attention of scouts with German club Hamburger SV. In 1988, Caligiuri moved on to SV Meppen in Germany's second division. He played there for two seasons, becoming one of the first Americans in the modern era to play in Europe. He later played for Hansa Rostock, where he helped the team win the last East German title before the country reunified in 1991. He would go on to play in MLS with the Columbus Crew and ended his career in 2001, with the Los Angeles Galaxy.

Caligiuri's looping left-footed volley from 30 yards out on the afternoon of November 19, 1989, silenced the home crowd in the 30th minute. It was a goal that forever changed the history of American soccer. The Americans, coached for this World Cup cycle by Bob Gansler, went into that game in Port of Spain knowing it had the crowd against it and a Trinidad and Tobago team that needed just a point to qualify for its first-ever World Cup. "It's been a long time, but it seems like yesterday," Caligiuri said in a 2005 interview with USSoccer.com. "I can literally still see the play and still feel the moment. I'm fortunate enough to still keep in touch with the guys on that team on a regular basis. It's been a fun ride."

A defender, Gansler had been a player himself and made five appearances for the senior U.S. team in 1968. He had also served as captain of the 1964 and 1968 Olympic teams, and at the 1967 Pan American Games. Gansler got into coaching after he retired in 1975. In the late 1980s, he

Photo 7.1.   U.S. coach Bob Gansler assembled a team of college players during 1990 World Cup qualifying. (Jon van Woerden)

Photo 7.2.   The United States starting lineup before defeating Trinidad & Tobago to qualify for its first World Cup in 40 years. (Jon van Woerden)

served as coach of the U.S. U-20 team, while also coaching the University of Wisconsin, Milwaukee men's soccer team. Appointed U.S. coach in 1989, Gansler had the difficult task of trying to get the Americans to a World Cup.

The last World Cup appearance by the United States had been in 1950. By defeating Trinidad and Tobago, the Americans joined Costa Rica— also reaching the World Cup for the first time—as CONCACAF's two representatives in the 24-team finals. Gansler's men had been clear underdogs during qualifying. The team, mostly consisting of college players and recent grads, pulled off the impossible. They may have been a bunch of obscure athletes at the time, but Gansler's roster now reads like a list of all-time U.S. greats.

The starting lineup featured lots of mullets—it was the 1980s, after all—with names like Tony Meola, John Harkes, and Tab Ramos. They didn't know it at the time, but these 20-somethings were pioneers. Meola, Harkes and Ramos, who grew up in New Jersey in the shadows of Giants Stadium on a steady diet of Cosmos games, would serve as the backbone of the national-team program for the next decade. "It was a big win for us. For me, it remains one of the biggest games I ever played in," said Meola. "That game got U.S. soccer back on the map. It put us back on the world stage."

Hasley Crawford Stadium was teeming with 30,000 red-clad fans. Trinidad and Tobago was playing at home under sunny skies. The government had even planned to declare the following day a national holiday—replete with huge celebrations—to coincide with the team qualifying. Everyone in Trinidad and Tobago, including the players, was certain they would advance to the finals. A week before the game, Trinidad and Tobago coach Gally Cummings, a former NASL player, boldly declared during a news conference, "After having seen the Americans, I am convinced that they will be no match for us." The Americans entered the match not having scored a goal in qualifying in 208 minutes.

Only a few dozen American fans made the journey to Port of Spain for the game, drowned out by the chants of the home crowd. Trinidad and Tobago only needed a draw (because of better scoring differential compared to the United States), but the Americans needed the win. To say it was an intimidating setting for the U.S. players would be an understatement. "I told my players, 'Pretend they are cheering for you,'" Gansler told the *New York Times* after the game. "In a way, I think we took energy from the fans."

In the end, the players were able to change the course of history for the national-team program. Immediately following the game, Fricker called the victory the "most important" for the federation and something the national-team program "needed very badly." The players chanted "It-a-ly" in the locker rooms, a postgame celebration that included lots of smiles and players showering one another with cans of cold beer. "Qualifying is hard business, and the fact that we would be an automatic qualifier for 1994 made it imperative that we get a World Cup under our belts before 1994 here in the States," said Bruce Murray, who started that day. "The U.S. team did well in 1994, and most of the key guys were veterans of 1990. To emphasize my point—where is Trinidad and Tobago today?"

Murray said qualifying for the 1990 World Cup and what the game meant to the future of American soccer is something he will never forget. "It was a monumental feat," he said, continuing,

We were under a lot of pressure. Bob Gansler went with college players over the old pros of the time. We then faltered and were able to pull it out in the final game. All those factors—including us hosting the 1994 World Cup—were all at play. We showed everyone we were legit, and we proved it on the field.

1990 WORLD CUP

The moment that had been 40 years in the making came together on December 9, 1989, at Rome's Palazzetto dello Sport for the World Cup draw. The United States was placed in Group A, based in Rome and Florence, alongside host nation Italy, Czechoslovakia, and Austria. For the Americans, a largely inexperienced collection of college grads lacking pro experience, it was a difficult group. Indeed, any group at this tournament would have been an uphill battle. For the United States, this tournament would be about gaining valuable experience ahead of the 1994 World Cup on home soil.

Gansler didn't mince words when speaking with the *New York Times* following the draw, but he also expressed optimism that the Americans could advance:

> We're up against the host nation, Italy, who are the big favorites to win the Cup, so that's going to be a very difficult challenge for my players—but

Photo 7.3. The U.S. players celebrate clinching a berth to the 1990 World Cup in the locker room. (Jon van Woerden)

something also to look forward to. Both Austria and Czechoslovakia are very capable teams with a lot of experience in the World Cup, so that gives them an edge over us. We have to set ourselves realistic goals, and history shows that three points from the first round is enough to advance to the next round.

Gansler and his players seemed unfazed by having to play Italy at Rome's Olympic Stadium. After all, the Americans had done the unthinkable against Trinidad and Tobago playing on the road. This would be a similar situation to what the Americans had faced before—magnified by a thousand given Italy's pedigree and status as favorites to win the tournament. "We'll have to take that into consideration during our preparation," Gansler told the *New York Times*, "but we feel that we overcame some of those problems when we beat Trinidad and Tobago in the vital final game of the qualifying round."

To prepare for the tournament, the United States played a series of friendlies. The occasional training camp, which, for decades, had been the method used to train ahead of games, was no longer going to work. The team operated more like a club side—it would even more so ahead of the 1994 World Cup—and embarked on a 12-game schedule before reaching Italy. The Americans participated in the Marlboro Cup in Miami, where they defeated Costa Rica, 2–0, on February 2, and lost to Colombia on penalty kicks after playing to a 1–1 draw. The United States was inconsistent, downing Bermuda, 1–0, on the road, and closing out the month with a 3–1 loss to the Soviet Union in Palo Alto, California. The U.S. team defeated Finland, 2–1, in Tampa on March 10, and followed that up by traveling to Europe to play a series of games there. It lost to Hungary, 2–0, in Budapest, and East Germany, 3–2, in East Berlin on March 28. The game had been a highly political affair given the Cold War history with the Eastern bloc nation. But the situation had been rapidly changing in Communist Europe. The Berlin Wall had already collapsed, and by 1991, Germany would be reunified.

The Americans defeated Iceland, 4–1, on April 8, and lost, 1–0, to Colombia on April 22, in Miami. Two final games were played in May before the team left for Europe. On May 5, the United States defeated Malta, 1–0, in Piscataway, New Jersey, before defeating Poland on May 9, in Hershey, Pennsylvania. In its final games before the World Cup, Gansler's team defeated Lichtenstein, 4–1, on May 30, before losing, 2–1, to Switzerland on June 2, in St. Gallen.

When the World Cup opened with Cameroon's 1–0 upset of defending champion Argentina in Milan, the U.S. players hoped that another shock result could be in the works when it faced Czechoslovakia in its first-round match in Florence. "Our guys felt good about what happened [against Argentina]," Gansler told reporters on the eve of the Czechoslovakia match. "They were rooting for Cameroon all along. I didn't have to belabor the point to them. They're an intelligent lot. They knew exactly the significance of what transpired."

The United States, however, had no player as gifted as Argentina's Diego Maradona to rely on should it get into a jam. The Americans were, after all, the youngest roster at the 24-team tournament. With an average age of just 24.2, Chris Henderson was the youngest of any of the 528 players at just 19 years old. "It was good to see that an underdog team can win," defender John Doyle told the *New York Times* when asked about Cameroon's win. "But I don't think Czechoslovakia would take us lightly. At least, I hope this hasn't made them extra careful of us." The hope was that Czechoslovakia would underestimate the Americans. Exactly the opposite would take place when the sides met on June 10, at the Stadio Comunale.

The United States had set up camp in the town of Tirrenia, just outside Pisa, ahead of its opener. The Americans appeared poised and confident, although the task ahead of them was a big one. With a smattering of American flags in the stands, mostly from members of the armed forces and their families stationed in Central Italy, Czechoslovakia—the bulk of its players hailing from storied club side Slavia Prague—was too much for the inexperienced Americans to handle. The outcome, a 5–1 embarrassment, confirmed what many had predicted at the outset: The Americans were not ready for such tough competition.

Caligiuri, whose goal against Trinidad and Tobago gave the United States its World Cup berth, scored the lone American goal in the 60th minute. The United States played the final 38 minutes with only 10 men after midfielder Eric Wynalda earned a red card following a hard tackle and proceeded to argue with Swiss referee Kurt Roethlisberger. "Obviously, our inexperience showed in a number of facets," he told reporters after the match. "We started out reasonably well—with a measure of self-confidence—but then we gave up a couple of soft goals. It was a good exhibition of what inexperience can do for you."

The goals had come fast and often, as the U.S. defense and Meola were unable to stop the hemorrhaging. Lubos Kubik, who played in the same stadium for Fiorentina, set up Tomas Skuhravy's first goal in the 26th minute. Kubik stole the ball in midfield and passed to Lubomir Moravcik, who beat out two defenders before passing to Skuhravy. His shot beat Meola from just 10 yards out. Michal Bilek helped Czechoslovakia double the lead before halftime, scoring in the 39th minute on a penalty kick called by Roethlisberger after defender Michael Windischmann fouled a player in the box. The second half was more of the same, as the Americans tried in vain to stop the strong Czechoslovakian offense. In the 50th minute, Skuhravy forced Meola to make a save that resulted in a corner kick. Ivan Hasek scored on a header on the ensuing play.

The only bright spot was the U.S. goal: Caligiuri took a pass from Murray in the midfield, dribbled into the box, and fired a strong shot that beat goalkeeper Jan Stejskal. But Czechoslovakia was undeterred, scoring another goal in the 78th minute, with Skuhravy redirecting a corner kick into the top of Meola's goal. Bilek missed a chance to score a second goal in the 87th minute after Czechoslovakia was awarded another penalty kick. John Harkes pulled down Hasek inside the penalty area. Bilek's chip shot was easily saved by Meola. Milan Luhovy scored in stoppage time for the 5–1 win. "I do believe that this team will regroup," Caligiuri told reporters after the game. "If we can learn from this, hopefully we can do better against Italy."

After the 5–1 rout by Czechoslovakia, the goal of the U.S. team in its second game was try to pull off an upset against Italy—or at least try to keep the score respectable. As both teams walked out of the tunnel at Rome's Olympic Stadium on June 15, they were greeted by some 73,000 flag-waving Italian fans. The rabid spectators created an intimidating atmosphere. For Meola, whose parents were Italian immigrants, the game represented a strange homecoming. He and teammates like Harkes and Ramos had grown up in the soccer hotbed of northern New Jersey on a steady diet of Italian soccer games on Sunday mornings via their satellite TVs. The same players they had idolized on television from afar were now standing alongside them for the playing of the national anthems. They had also spent their weekends in the parking lot at Giants Stadium kicking around a ball during tailgate parties for New York Cosmos games. Pelé and Giorgio Chinaglia were their idols. They had gone from watching players who had been at a World Cup to being the ones taking part in the world's biggest sporting event. Indeed, for many on Gansler's team, it was the first time they had ever played in front of such a large crowd.

By all accounts this was to be a mismatch. Italy had won three World Cups entering the tournament and in Serie A featured the world's best and most competitive domestic league. With striker Salvatore "Toto" Schillaci leading the way as a super-sub and a defense that boasted sweeper Franco Baresi, the versatile Paolo Maldini, and the gritty Giuseppe Bergomi, the U.S. attack had little chance. Italy's entire roster was Serie A-based, while the U.S. team listed seven college players. Only three players—Peter Vermes, Christopher Sullivan, and Caligiuri—were under contract overseas. "I was playing at the University of San Francisco, [Italy midfielder Roberto] Donadoni was playing at AC Milan," Doyle told MLSSoccer.com in 2014. "Our entire payroll was one Italian player."

Gansler again went with Murray up front—a player he had relied on for nearly two years—and didn't let the Czechosolvakia loss change his

Photo 7.4. Peter Vermes (right) takes on a trio of players in the U.S.'s 1-0 loss to Italy at the 1990 World Cup. (Jon van Woerden)

mind. "It was a different time," said Murray. "I give Bob Gansler much credit for sticking with me and with his game plan," he added. "Now, a coach will pull the plug on a striker if he has one bad game. With me, [Gansler] gave me the confidence and trust to succeed."

While Murray was tasked with scoring the goals, Meola and the defense were there to try and stop them. But what had been an expected rout turned into a respectable loss. The United States would lose, 1–0, with the Italians dominating long stretches of play but frustrated by an American defense that tried its best to keep the ball out of its half. The Americans played like a unified block, something Gansler had hoped for after the humiliation of that first loss had transformed into anger in the U.S. camp. Players turned on one another in the days following the 5–1 defeat, as some were angry at Wynalda for his red card, which had left the Americans a player short for much of the second half. But Wynalda, ineligible to play against Italy due to the red card's one-match ban, said he felt vindicated after a FIFA official had come to his defense. In an interview in the Swiss newspaper *Berner Zeitung*, Joseph Blatter, then-general secretary of FIFA, said Roethlisberger had been "clearly too harsh" in making the call. Wynalda, in an interview with the *New York Times* following the Italy match, said, "I'm glad in a way that somebody finally said something in my favor. I have always felt it was a little unjustified."

As for the Italy game, the United States went down early after Giuseppe Giannini, a midfielder for AS Roma, gave the home crowd something to cheer about in the 11th minute. Giannini beat both Harkes and Windischmann, and then got the ball past Meola with a left-footed shot after going at him one-on-one. His goal gave Italy the 1–0 lead, and the floodgates seemed to be open. Italy's three major sports dailies had predicted a *goleada*—a goal-fest—against the Americans. It certainly seemed to be the start of one. Twenty-two minutes later, Caligiuri fouled Nicola Berti in the box, setting up a penalty kick for Gianluca Vialli. But the Italian striker shot to the left, and the ball hit the base of the post, as Meola had guessed to his right. "That was the turning point of the game," defender Desmond Armstrong told the *Los Angeles Times* after the game. "It showed us that those guys are human, that we could play with them." To make up for its technical abilities and lack of experience on such a huge stage, the United States put on a very American performance, full of hustle and physical play.

As the United States frustrated the Italians, Gansler's men almost tied the score. In the 68th minute, Murray lined up to take a free kick about 25 yards out. Walter Zenga could barely keep the ball out of the goal, pushing it away. That's when Vermes charged at the ball, getting off another hard shot. The ball got through Zenga's legs, but it was cleared off the line by an Italian defender. "Honestly, the ball didn't deserve to go in," Vermes told MLSSoccer.com in 2014, "because in the end they played better than we did. They had a lot more chances. We were surviving and hanging on in the game, but we truly didn't deserve to tie them. But I will say that we saved face a little bit." After the game, Gansler felt the same way when addressing reporters. "I feel we earned a little bit of respect," he said of the 1–0 loss. "I feel very good for my team because we came back from the ashes. We've got to feel like the Phoenix tonight."

Although not mathematically eliminated, the Americans would need to win in its final group match versus Austria by five goals and hope for a series of developments in other games to be considered one of the best third-place teams. The chances of advancing were slim, but they existed, and Gansler's players planned to go into the game hoping for a win. "The mathematical possibilities would require [Albert] Einstein at his best to figure out," Gansler told the *New York Times* on the eve of the June 19 game in Florence. "We just have to focus on a good performance to try to get the two points that are still out there. Obviously, we have to score a ton of goals to advance."

American players were also out to impress European scouts who might be in the stands while looking ahead to the 1994 World Cup. Some players had already received calls, and Gansler told reporters he was in favor of American players signing with pro teams and trying to make a go at it in the competitive environment Europe's domestic leagues offered. But the primary task at hand was trying to put together a good showing versus an Austria team that featured Anton "Toni" Polster, one of the game's most lethal strikers. The outcome for the United States would be similar to its previous two matches. The game was a physical affair (referee Jamal al-Sharif of Syria issued nine cautions and a red card that left Austria down a player), as the Americans put in another gritty performance. The 2–1 defeat ensured that the Americans would end 0–3, with two goals scored and eight conceded.

Down 2–0, Murray scored the only U.S. goal in the 83rd minute after goalkeeper Klaus Lindenberger had stopped two consecutive shots from Harkes and Vermes. But when Vermes got the ball back off the deflection, he passed it to Ramos, who chipped it to Murray for the goal. It was a nifty play and one of the few bright spots for a team that showed some improvement with each game. "Obviously, we're disappointed. We came here to gather the two points for a victory, and we felt we had the ability to do it," Gansler told reporters after the game. "Unfortunately, we came up short. With the second and third games, though, I feel we showed that the difference between nations who are perpetually here and those like ourselves is not as great as some believe."

JOHN HARKES

John Harkes was born on March 8, 1967, in Kearney, New Jersey. The midfielder played in the English Premier League, the first American to play there, and was a staple of the U.S. midfield throughout the 1990s.

Career: Harkes's career was full of records. His move to Sheffield Wednesday in 1990, made him the first U.S.-born player in England's top pro league. In his first season, Harkes's goal against Derby County—a 35-yard shot past England international Peter Shilton—earned him the English "Goal of the Year" award. In the 1990–1991 season, Harkes became the second American (after Bill Regan in 1948–1949) to play at Wembley when Sheffield Wednesday won the 1991 Football League Cup, 1–0, against Manchester United. That year, Sheffield Wednesday also won promotion to the First Division, now known as the Premier League. In 1993, Harkes became the only American to score in a League Cup final, a 2–1 loss to Arsenal. He was transferred to Derby County (1993–1995) before making just 12 appearances during the 1995–1996 season with West Ham.

In 1996, Harkes returned to the United States and signed with MLS. He was allocated to DC United. That year, he led the team to both the MLS Cup and the U.S. Open Cup. He led the team to another MLS title in 1997, then helped DC United become the first MLS team to win the CONCACAF Champions Cup and an upset win against Brazil's Vasco Da Gama in the Copa Interamericana. At the end of the 1998 MLS season, Harkes returned to England. He returned to MLS in 1999, playing three seasons with the New England Revolution before being traded to the Columbus Crew. He retired in 2003.

National Team: Harkes played for the United States in the 1990 and 1994 World Cups. In 1996, coach Steve Samspon named Harkes "Captain for Life"; however, he was left off the 1998 World Cup roster, a decision that was not explained at the time. The bitterness that ensued led to Harkes writing a book entitled *Captain for Life: And Other Temporary Assignments*, released in 1999. In the book, Harkes criticized Sampson. He wrote, "I can't think of one thing that Steve did right in the months leading up to the (1998) World Cup." In 2010, Harkes's former teammate Eric Wynalda claimed an alleged affair between Harkes and Wynalda's wife Amy led to the decision to leave him off the squad. Harkes made 90 appearances for the United States, scoring six goals. He was elected to the National Soccer Hall of Fame in 2005.

Coaching: Harkes worked as a TV analyst for ABC/ESPN from 2006 to 2011. In 2006, he became an assistant coach with the New York Red Bulls. In 2015, Harkes was named head coach of FC Cincinnati, an expansion team in the United Soccer League. He was fired in 2017.

Family: Harkes and his wife Cindi have three children, Ian, Lilly, and Lauren. Ian also won a Hermann Trophy and currently plays for DC United.

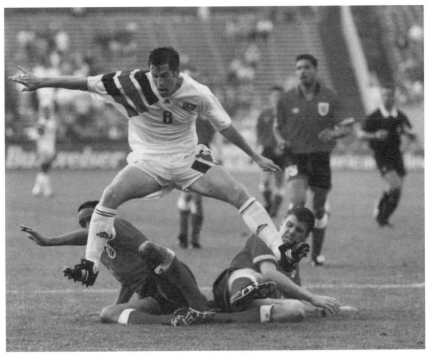

Photo 7.5.   John Harkes in action during U.S. Cup '93. (Jon van Woerden)

1991 CONCACAF GOLD CUP

The Gold Cup was the region's new way of crowning a continental champion. No longer tied to World Cup qualifying, the tournament was made to resemble the Euros or Copa America. The favorites going into the competition were Mexico, back from its suspension; Honduras; Costa Rica; and, for the first time, the United States, now led by their new coach, Yugoslavian-born Velibor Milutinovic. He had coached Costa Rica a year earlier at the World Cup and came with a wealth of experience and knowledge of the game in Europe and the Americas.

Although his English was remedial, "Bora," as he was affectionately called, made himself understood by players and reporters alike. Dubbed a "miracle worker," it would be his task to bring improvement to a U.S. team not respected in the region, let alone the world. The charismatic Milutinovic was not afraid to try new things and brought with him an unprecedented amount of passion and enthusiasm for the job. His playfulness put the players at ease but also made them want to work for him. With U.S. Soccer and its president, Alan Rothenberg, committed to bankrolling the national team in the way other federations throughout the world traditionally had, there were no limits to how far this group could go.

Photo 7.6.   U.S. coach Bora Milutinovic was tasked with helping the team build its program for the 1994 World Cup. (Jon van Woerden)

While a new pro league was still a few years away—one of the preconditions FIFA had placed on the United States for granting them World Cup hosting rights—the players found ways to remain fit and challenged. Some, like Harkes, who signed with English club Sheffield Wednesday after the World Cup, found their way to Europe. The bulk of the team played in the American Professional Soccer League, a newly formed circuit that had come about following the 1989 merger with the Western Soccer League. Although the APSL folded in 1996, it had featured 22 clubs at its height in 1990, and kept players employed before MLS was formed. It served as a de facto Division I league, even though it catered to a few thousand fans per game and had little to no television exposure. The MISL was still limping around, but even indoor soccer suffered the indifference the NASL ultimately felt. The league changed its name to MSL—dropping the word *indoor*—in the hopes of functioning in the future as an outdoor league. It would never happen, and the league folded in 1992, its legacy being that it served as this country's only national soccer league at a time when the NASL had left a major void. Nonetheless, the game's purists were happy to see the MISL vanish. In its place was an enthusiasm and growing support for the national team.

The Gold Cup was the perfect place for the United States to show that it was for real. A program that was still rebuilding post–World Cup, it featured many of the players who had gained experience in Italy—like Meola, Ramos, and Harkes. "That was one of the first times that, as a national team player, going into a tournament, that I felt we were there to drive the play and push our game on other teams," said Vermes, who served as team captain at the time. "A lot of times prior and leading up to that tournament, we were just trying to hang with these guys, as opposed to dominating the game. I felt that's what we did throughout the tournament, including the game against Mexico in the semifinal."

The United States won its group, defeating Trinidad and Tobago, 2–1, Guatemala, 3–0, and Costa Rica, 3–2, to advance to the semifinals. The most thrilling moment from the first round was Marcelo Balboa's bicycle-kick goal in the final minute to give the United States a comeback victory over Trinidad and Tobago. Balboa, who would play 128 times for the national team, was a standout defender who had started his career with the APSL's San Francisco Blackhawks. In 1995, he became the first American player to break the 100-appearance record for national-team games. A key member of the 1994 World Cup squad, Balboa would play two seasons in Mexico with León and go on to a successful six seasons in MLS, four of those seasons with the Colorado Rapids. "Playing in 1994 [at the World Cup] was also a great feeling," said Balboa. "I'll never forget that!"

Once in the semis, the Americans were pitted against Mexico (who finished second to Honduras on goal differential in the other group) for a July 5 date at Memorial Coliseum before a pro-Mexico crowd of 41,000. It was in the semifinals that the United States did the unthinkable by defeating Mexico, and this time the video evidence could not be hidden. It was done in plain sight—a feat that lives on to this day on YouTube—and to much fanfare. The Americans had a slight edge. Milutinovic had coached Mexico in the 1986 World Cup, getting them into the quarterfinals. Beloved by Mexican soccer fans, he had mixed emotions going into the game. "It was a really great experience for me. I was very proud of the players," said Milutinovic. "The Mexicans [in the crowd] respected me, and they were happy for me. It was great to see."

In the end, Doyle's goal in the 48th minute and a second from Vermes in the 64th would seal the win. "I think the success of that Gold Cup gave us a really big jump forward," said Vermes. "It said that we could be a dominant force in CONCACAF and gave us a lot of momentum moving towards the next World Cup." As captain, Vermes said he felt the extra pressure of trying to keep the players focused throughout the tournament. The lineup featured many players who would go on to be the core of the 1994 U.S. World Cup squad, including Meola (who was named 1991 Gold Cup MVP) and Wynalda. For Vermes, the victory over Mexico—and the win over Honduras two days later, 4–3, on penalties following a scoreless draw in the final—was the start of the ongoing run by the U.S. team as an elite squad in CONCACAF. "We had been dominated by Mexico for many years up to that point, and I think the commanding victory and the way we approached the game and the way we played, I think it surprised them quite a bit," he said, adding,

> I think it was the beginning step in this dominance we've had over them in CONCACAF for many years now. I think it was the beginning of letting Mexico know that there was another team in CONCACAF that they were going to have to deal with, and I think since then we have risen to the top and become that dominant force.

1992 U.S. CUP

As host, the United States automatically qualified for the World Cup. To stay fit and get the team games, the newly rebranded USSF, now known as U.S. Soccer, created a new tournament. The 1992 U.S. Cup was a four-team round-robin competition featuring three other national teams. In its first edition, U.S. Soccer invited Italy, Ireland, and Portugal. The competition would not only keep the players, most of whom were in full-time residency in Mission Viejo, California, under contract with U.S. Soccer, but also generate revenue. Italy, Ireland, and Portugal would draw immigrants to see their beloved national teams. Once again, this was not about creating a home-field advantage for the United States. Getting games and gaining experience was much more important at this stage of the national team's development. The United States would go on to win two games—versus Ireland (3–1) and Portugal (1–0)—while drawing Italy, 1–1, in the final group match to win the tournament.

Effective man-to-man marking, a tight defense, and the ability to set an offside trap showed that the Americans had gone from naïve to respectable. Much of the credit went to Milutinovic and his roster, which incorporated several naturalized players, including striker Roy Wegerle of South Africa and defender Thomas Dooley of Germany. U.S. Soccer had hired Milutinovic to shore up a weak defense and bring some professionalism to the team. At the 1992 U.S. Cup, the team demonstrated it had both a strong defense and professionalism as it geared up for the 1994 World Cup.

Photo 7.7.   Milutinovic and his players during a training session in Chicago. (Jon van Woerden

   In the decisive game on June 6, at Chicago's Soldier Field, a Harkes goal in the 23rd minute canceled out Italy's Roberto Baggio, who had put his side ahead after just two minutes. "We had to seize the moment," Harkes told the *New York Times* after the game. "This match was being shown around the world." Harkes ended as the tournament's top scorer, with two goals.

1992 KING FAHD CUP

By virtue of being crowned CONCACAF champion, the United States, along with the other continental winners, were invited by Saudi Arabia to participate in the King Fahd Cup, also known as the Intercontinental Champions Cup. The tournament would later attain FIFA's endorsement and morph into the Confederations Cup. The four-team competition featured Argentina, the Copa America champion; Saudi Arabia, the host nation and defending Asian champion; Ivory Coast, winner of the Africa Cup of Nations; and the United States.

Milutinovic brought with him a full squad, including Meola in goal and Ramos in the midfield. On October 15, in Riyadh, the United States took on Saudi Arabia in front of 70,000 people at King Fahd II Stadium, marking the first time the Americans had played a game in a Middle Eastern nation. The hosts would win, 3–0, after the Americans had been able to leave the Saudis off the board in the first half. Four days later, the United States would play for third place, again in Riyadh, downing Ivory Coast, 5–2. It would be two goals from Murray late in the match that would push the Americans to victory. Murray, along with Argentina's Gabriel Batistuta, would finish the tournament as joint top scorers, with two goals each. That maiden tournament had gone well for the Americans and given them another stage on which to show off their improvement in front of a global audience.

1993 COPA AMERICA

A year before the World Cup, U.S. Soccer organized the 1993 U.S. Cup, this time inviting a trio of former World Cup champions—Brazil, Germany, and England. The tournament would serve as a perfect dress rehearsal for the World Cup, a test for logistics, stadium security, and troublesome fans. While the Americans would finish third, their 2–0 victory against the English on June 9, at Foxboro Stadium near Boston, proved impressive. "Our national team has passed from childhood," Hank Steinbrecher, U.S. Soccer's General Secretary, told the *New York Times* on the eve of the tournament. "We're an adolescent. At times, we can stand with adults. At other times, we can slip back." Against England, the Americans clearly played the role of adult. Goals from Dooley and defender Alexi Lalas, who had come on as a second-half sub, would force London's *The Sun* newspaper, to go with the headline, "Yanks 2, Planks 0."

The summer, however, would be highlighted by the United States being invited to the Copa America. Along with Mexico, the United States would get the chance to test itself against the best teams from South America in a tournament that mattered. The United States, fielding a diluted squad in an effort to rest players for the upcoming Gold Cup, would be challenged after being seeded in Group A, with host nation Ecuador, Uruguay, and Venezuela. The Americans would finish fourth in the group, going 0–1–2, their only point coming after a 3–3 draw against Venezuela on June 22, in Quito. Even that match revealed a major weakness: an inability to maintain a lead. Up 1–0 following Dominic Kinnear's goal in the 51st minute, Venezuela would score three unanswered goals.

1993 CONCACAF GOLD CUP

Milutinovic's men would cruise to the final. Milutinovic believed the more games the United States could play before the World Cup, the better. The spring and summer of 1993 would prove to be the most arduous in the team's history. By year's end, the Americans would play 34 games, posting a 10–11–13 record. The Americans played their best soccer at the Gold Cup. Milutinovic continued to encourage his team to work on refining and improving its defense. Although it made for low-scoring games (the offense was not firing on all cylinders), the United States, the defending Gold Cup champion, reached the final after defeating Costa Rica, 1–0, in Dallas. A goal from Cle Kooiman in extra time won the game.

The action moved farther south, where Mexico City would play host to the championship game on July 25. The altitude of Estadío Azteca—along with the loud and boisterous Mexican fans—ensured the Mexicans had home-field advantage. The Americans needed an offensive spark if they hoped to have a chance. In fact, the team had only scored five goals in four games entering the match. On the day of the game, Mexican newspaper *El Nacional* ran with the headline, "For Revenge," a reference to the team's 2–0 loss to the United States two years earlier.

Unfortunately for the Americans, that goal drought would persist. With 120,000 fans cheering on their team, the Mexicans returned to form, romping over the United States, 4–0. The United States, intimidated by the crowd, was without Ramos, sidelined due to yellow-card accumulation. The Mexicans, Copa America runners-up just a month earlier to winner Argentina, unleashed their attack early, forcing the Americans to go down, 2–0, at halftime. The second Mexican score, an own goal by defender Desmond Armstrong that got past Meola, put the game out of reach for the United States. The team was dejected, but there was still so much more to play for. The World Cup was on the horizon, and it was there, at home, that the U.S. team needed to get results. It wasn't just something that would benefit the team. It had the potential of also boosting the sport in the United States.

1994 WORLD CUP

World Cup organizers wasted no time getting the ball rolling on the tournament. Promotion for the event began in 1991, and American soccer officials saw it as their duty to promote the sport. A key component of this was improving the national team. Organizers, including Rothenberg, had the chore of trying to convince an apathetic American public that the World Cup was coming to their shores. A Harris poll conducted just three weeks before the start of the World Cup did little to quell those fears. Although ticket packages had sold out six months earlier, it was anyone's guess what the atmosphere would be like. The poll found that 56 percent of those surveyed said they were not interested in watching any World Cup games on TV, with 65 percent saying they were not interested in attending. If that wasn't bad enough, only 38 percent knew that the World Cup was a soccer tournament.

"In 1992 and 1993, we played home games and still had to play in front of fans that were rooting for the other country," said Dooley. "Actually, it felt like we always had an away game. I think the first time we filled up the stadium with Americans was at the U.S. Cup in 1993, and then it got better and better from there." In the end, the 1994 World Cup would be remembered for being very successful, while still holding the record for the best average attendance for a World Cup, at 68,991 per game.

U.S. Soccer spent the post-World Cup years 1990s strengthening its national-team program. With no pro league, staging friendlies against other nations was the only real way for American players to gain experience. Under Milutinovic, the team had seen some improvement. At the same time, a number of American players had gotten the chance to play abroad: Wynalda, Ramos, and Harkes had inked deals with European clubs and were testing themselves on a weekly basis in league games. Wynalda signed with FC Saarbrucken in Germany, Ramos spent time with Real Betis in Spain, and Harkes had a successful run with Sheffield Wednesday in England.

Winning the Gold Cup in 1991 and putting on strong showings in the U.S. Cup provided proof that the United States could occasionally compete with some of the world's best. What the team needed was more consistency. That would come with time. For now, Milutinovic had the task of trying to improve the team at a rapid pace. He began the arduous process of building the team from the ground up.

By 1993, the U.S. team had played 34 internationals, going 10–11–13. There was room for improvement, but Milutinovic had done a lot to bring respect and credibility to a program that, just a decade earlier, had been in shambles. The future of soccer in the United States depended on whether the national team could make a decent showing at the World Cup. Although winning the World Cup was not an attainable goal, the least the team could aim for was advancing to the knockout round.

The United States was drawn into Group A as the top-seed, given that it was the host nation. That same American public that appeared uninterested in the World Cup on the eve of the tournament would quickly change their minds. Milutinovic's team was prepared to deliver victories and almost did so in its first game. The United States opened on June 8, at the Pontiac Silverdome outside Detroit, against Switzerland, in front of 73,425 spectators in the first World Cup game ever played indoors. More than 2,000 trays of natural grass grown in California were installed at the venue, an experiment organizers had put into use the previous year at the U.S. Cup, when Germany and England played the tournament's final game there; however, for the U.S.–Switzerland game, the suffocating heat inside the domed stadium reached 106 degrees—but did nothing to stop the teams from putting on a good show.

The situation didn't look good for the Americans early on when the Swiss took a 1–0 lead after only five minutes. Thomas Dooley brought down Alain Sutter just outside the penalty box, and Georges Bregy converted the 19-yard free kick with a curling shot that made its way past the American wall and over Meola's head into the right corner of the net. The U.S. response was feeble at first but grew more convincing as the half wore on. In the 45th minute, Harkes was taken down by Swiss midfielder Ciriaco Sforza, setting up a free kick for the Americans about 30 yards away from the goal. Wynalda, who had woken up that morning covered in hives after suffering an allergic reaction to something he had eaten the prior night, lined up to take the kick. His shot curled over the wall and hit the underside of the crossbar before finding the back of the net just as goalkeeper Marco Pascolo tried to put a hand on it. The crowd cheered, and the U.S. players rejoiced. The Americans, although not totally impressive, had earned a 1–1 tie and a point.

Next up for the United States was mighty Colombia at the Rose Bowl. The Colombians, laden with talent, had lost to Romania, 3–1, in their first game and were desperate to get at least a point to stay alive. The 93,194 fans who attended the game would witness history. To everyone's surprise, the Americans took the lead in the 32nd minute, when Harkes sent a cross from the left across the middle of the field about 15 yards away from the goal. The pass—intended for Earnie Stewart—never got to the speedy player. Instead, the ball was intercepted by Colombian defender Andres Escobar, who mistakenly deflected the ball into his own net. Goalkeeper Oscar Cordoba never had a chance to stop it. The own goal left Escobar and his teammates stunned while the Americans celebrated. The goal would forever leave a dark footnote.

Photo 7.8.   Eric Wynalda celebrates his spectacular free kick versus Switzerland at the 1994 World Cup. (Jon van Woerden)

A few days after Colombia had returned home from the tournament, Escobar was gunned down following a fight with a group of men in a suburb of Medellin. He was shot 12 times as the men shouted, "Goal!" each time the trigger was pulled.

As for the game, Milutinovic's team had caught the break they needed and were safely in control of the situation. The most indelible image of the match, if not the tournament, was Marcelo Balboa's bicycle kick. The shot didn't go in, but that didn't matter to the pro-U.S. crowd, which went bonkers at everything the Americans did that afternoon. The Colombians attempted a comeback in the second half, but playmaker Carlos Valderrama, who did a good job controlling the midfield, could not get his teammates in the game. The United States had momentum on its side, and Stewart, unstoppable on the right flank, made it 2–0 in the 52nd minute after outrunning two defenders to the ball before hitting a hard shot that bounced into the goal. Dooley, who had played sweeper against Switzerland and got himself involved offensively, hung back on defense this time, while Balboa and Alexi Lalas, with his red mop of hair and goatee, shut down the Colombians' feeble effort to get off any shots on goal.

The Colombians could do nothing until the 89th minute, when Adolfo Valencia scored. But the goal was ultimately little consolation for the Colombians, who were officially eliminated. The Americans had pulled off a 2–1 upset and now had a real chance of advancing to the knockout stage. The crowd erupted at the sound of the final whistle, and the Americans celebrated on the field like they had won the trophy. Meola danced around the field draped in an American flag, while his teammates waved to the crowd and hugged one another. The win was the first World Cup victory since the United States had defeated England in 1950. If that win had been a fluke that barely got any attention at home, this victory was for real and was expected to help propel soccer to the status of major sport in the country.

"During the World Cup in 1994, on the way from the hotel to the daily training sessions, we had to pass some basketball fields. I always looked out the windows and was sad. I thought, 'Come on guys, the World Cup is here in the United States, and you don't even know it or care for it,'" Dooley said. "After we won against Colombia at the Rose Bowl, the next day we passed the court, and all of the basketball players stopped playing immediately, walked to the street, and applauded and cheered for us. That was an unbelievable feeling for me."

The Americans were poised to win the group with a victory in their final group game, but they lost to Romania, 1–0, on June 26, playing in front of 93,869 onlookers at the sunbaked Rose Bowl. The Romanians attacked from the start and were rewarded in the 18th minute, when defender Dan Petrescu put the ball past Meola. Harkes received a yellow card, his second in three games, making him unavailable for the next game. Harkes's card did not sit well with Balboa, who went over to the New Jersey native and reprimanded him. Balboa even shoved Harkes, who then pushed him back. The scene wasn't pretty and was a sign that team unity had begun to fall apart. The loss, however, was only a minor setback. The Americans had reached the knockout round.

The Americans faced Brazil on the afternoon of July 4, in Palo Alto, California. The 84,147 fans in attendance at Stanford Stadium were decked out in red, white, and blue to celebrate both Independence Day and the team so many throughout the country had learned to love in the span of just a few weeks. To avoid his players being in awe of the situation they found themselves in, Milutinovic had given them some simple advice on the eve of the game: "Please don't ask for autographs." With that, the U.S. team—a squad no one expected could get this far—was among the 16 best in the world. "I've been [with the national team] seven years; when I started, we weren't ranked in the top 100 in the world," Meola told the *New York Times*.

Even though Brazilian fans were also out in force, chants of "U-S-A! U-S-A!" filled the stadium once the game got underway. The Americans gained a one-man advantage in the 43rd minute after Leonardo's bone-crunching elbow found Ramos's face. The midfielder hit the ground, while Leonardo was shown a red card. But the Brazilians pressured

Photo 7.9. Postage stamps featuring the U.S. national team were released to commemorate the 1994 World Cup. (USPS/DepositPhotos)

the U.S. goal the entire time, until Bebeto, off a sensational pass from Romário, managed to score in the 72nd minute. Milutinovic, fearing a rout, had set up a defensive strategy. The plan of absorbing pressure and trying to score on the counterattack had not worked. Bebeto's goal would be the game-winner, and the dream of going further at the World Cup would have to be deferred. "With all due respect to the American team, which is a great team, I think Brazil dominated the game," Romário told reporters after the match. "Just one ball went in, but with a little luck, two or three others could have as well."

Overall, the United States earned universal praise for what it had been able to achieve. For the first time, the national team had triggered the passion of American fans. After the Brazil loss, Milutinovic declared that soccer had a "bright future." At the same time, American players had been noticed by other teams. By far the biggest signing was that of the colorful Lalas, who joined Padova in Serie A, becoming the first American in almost 60 years to play in Italy.

1995 COPA AMERICA

A subsequent invitation to the Copa America tournament gave the United States another chance to test itself against some of the best teams in South America. Following Milutinovic's defensive tactics, this was a chance for former U.S. assistant coach Steve Sampson, who replaced Milutinovic as coach, to show that the United States could also be an attack-minded side. By the time the tournament was over, the Americans had gained newfound respectability, and U.S. Soccer had been thrust in the spotlight once again following the 1994 World Cup. The tournament was hosted by Uruguay, and Sampson brought with him a strong roster.

The Americans opened the tournament on July 8, with a 2–1 win against Chile. Wynalda scored both goals at the Estadio Parque Artigas. Two days later, the Americans lost, 1–0, to Bolivia. With Bolivia losing to Argentina in their opening game, this created a scenario that was unfavorable to the United States, as they needed to defeat Argentina, a team ranked eighth in the world at the time, in the final group game.

The United States used a platoon system in goal, with Brad Friedel and Kasey Keller in contention for the starting role. Meola had fallen out of favor at this point, although he continued to play well in the ensuing years and was named MLS MVP, Goalkeeper of the Year, and MLS Cup MVP in 2000, after helping the Kansas City Wizards win the title. The two goalkeepers had alternated starts in the previous two first-round matches, with Keller in goal against Argentina. The Argentines—still coping with the end of the Diego Maradona era—did not need a win to advance, and coach Daniel Passarella rested most of his regulars for the game. The United States won the game. Goals by Frank Klopas, Alexi Lalas, and Eric Wynalda propelled the Americans to a 3–0 shutout. The victory ranks as not only the biggest upset of that decade, but also one of the biggest in team history. Soccer historian Roger Allaway ranks it as the biggest. "There are lots of candidates, but I think my choice would be the 3–0 win over Argentina in the 1995 Copa America," he said.

For Sampson, the victory was a culmination of months of hard work. In a 2013 interview with USSoccer.com, he said,

> Our last match in group play against Argentina became a very important match for us. We had to beat Argentina or at the very least tie them in order for us to go on. On that day, the U.S. team had one of its best performances in history. . . . One of the great moments was when Diego Maradona came down to the locker room and greeted our U.S. players and told them how proud he was of not only the fact that they beat Argentina, but of the quality of soccer that they played.

Sampson—nicknamed "Uncle Sam"—had never played the game, but he was a coaching staple for years. He was an assistant coach in the early 1980s at UCLA and, in 1986, began a four-year stint at Santa Clara University. In 1993, he was named an assistant to Milutinovic. In addition to his coaching duties, Sampson also worked as an administrator, as vice president of competition management for the 1994 World Cup organizing committee.

Sampson was given the job of coaching the team full time in 1995, after a string of positive results. Milutinovic had resigned in 1995 (according to U.S. Soccer at the time), although the coach claimed he had been fired. U.S. Soccer tried in vain to sign a big-name foreign coach—Carlos Queiroz of Portugal and Carlos Alberto Parreria of Brazil were up for the role—while Sampson wore the interim tag. Parreira had guided Brazil to the World Cup in 1994, and was seen as a leading candidate. In the end, Sampson would get the job after a series of impressive victories that year, including a 4–0 win against Mexico at the 1995 U.S. Cup. The U.S. Cup would be contested four more times, with the U.S. winning just one edition in 2000. He would be the first full-time, native-born American to coach the national team. "Obviously, we were impressed with the results, but we were much more impressed by the way the results were obtained," Alan Rothenberg said during a conference call with reporters in August 1995. He continued,

> Steve really did epitomize the American style. He had an opportunity, he went for it, and his players responded. Even in the games that we lost, we played a style that made me proud to watch and be a part of. The way he did it was probably more impressive than the results themselves.

The Americans didn't stop with the win versus Argentina. In the quarterfinals, the team defeated Mexico, 4–1, in a shootout, after playing to a scoreless draw with Friedel in goal. The Americans had played the first four games of the tournament in Paysandu, where the locals had adopted the United States as their team. In the semifinals, the Americans played Brazil in Maldonado on July 20, in a rematch of the World Cup game a year earlier. Again, the Americans lost, 1–0, this time on a goal by Aldair after 13 minutes. The team would finish fourth, losing to Colombia, 4–1, on July 22, at the Estadio Campus Municipal in Maldonado. Sampson did not play Harkes, Dooley, Balboa, or Wynalda in a game that meant little.

Despite its great showing, the team did not produce the frenzy back home that more recent national-team exploits had. The Internet was still in its infancy, and Copa America matches had only aired on pay-per-view. Nonetheless, the Americans had come of age. With the surprise performance in the 1994 World Cup and the strong showing in the 1995 Copa, any lingering doubt about the quality of American soccer had finally been laid to rest in the eyes of the world. The future looked brighter than ever for the national team.

1998 WORLD CUP QUALIFYING

After hosting a World Cup—and receiving an automatic spot in the finals—the United States embarked on qualifying for the 1998 World Cup in France. CONCACAF was awarded a third spot in the finals after the tournament had been expanded from 24 teams to 32. Qualifying would consist of four rounds, the final one a six-team round-robin tournament known as the Hexagonal. The Americans started off in the third round, placed in Group 1 with Costa Rica, Trinidad and Tobago, and Guatemala in 1996. The United States would finish first, going 4–1–1 to reach the Hexagonal.

The final round featured the best teams from the region, including perennial powerhouse Mexico and upstarts such as Jamaica. The United States featured such veterans as Meola, Harkes, and Ramos. It also had in its lineup the likes of Eddie Pope, a hard-nosed defender; a finesse midfielder in Claudio Reyna; and a more mature striker in Eric Wynalda. Nicknamed "Waldo" by his teammates, Wynalda, along with Brian Mc-Bride, was now the team's go-to striker. He had made history in 1996, scoring the first-ever goal in an MLS match. The new league would ultimately become home to the bulk of the roster that would go on to play at the World Cup, a team that included former indoor star Preki. Sixteen

MLS players on Sampson's 22-man roster would travel to France in the summer of 1998.

Sampson was excited about the prospect of guiding the team at a World Cup. He told the *Los Angeles Times,*

> I accept the challenge with the full knowledge and responsibility that this is a very critical time for soccer in the United States. We have to continue playing a good brand of soccer, continue to enthuse the U.S. public, continue to show that we can compete with the best teams in the world. This is a great challenge, and by no stretch of the imagination is it an easy task, but I think we have the players who can compete at the highest level. And I think we have the players . . . and the foundation of a team that will play extremely well in France and hopefully better than we did last year in the U.S. World Cup.

In qualifying, the United States would benefit from home-field advantage but struggle on the road. CONCACAF was known for being the region where winning on the road was toughest. Whether it was playing in dilapidated stadiums in Central America in front of coin-tossing fans or on poor fields on a tiny Caribbean island, Sampson's team had to muster all its talent and guile to try and win. The Americans looked to be on the brink of elimination but turned their fortunes around in the final month of the Hex.

A scoreless draw against Mexico on November 2, 1997, at Estadío Azteca, and a 3–0 road victory seven days later versus Canada in Vancouver, thanks to goals from Reyna and Wegerle, secured the team's passage to France in 1998. On the final day of qualifying, the United States posted a 4–2 win against El Salvador in the friendly confines of Foxboro Stadium. Two McBride goals that day in Boston were enough to propel the team to victory, putting it second in the Hex, behind Mexico and ahead of Jamaica, who had qualified for its first-ever World Cup. "It was important to finish on a high," Harkes told the *Boston Globe* after the game. "We needed to finish in style, and that's what we did."

1998 CONCACAF GOLD CUP

The tournament's fourth edition took place in February that year, so as to not coincide with the World Cup. Although Mexico would lift the trophy, defeating the United States, 1–0, on February 15, at the Los Angeles Memorial Coliseum, it was the semifinal played there five days earlier that made history.

CONCACAF decided to invite Brazil to the tournament that year in an effort to bring some attention to the Gold Cup. It also allowed CONCACAF teams, like the United States, to measure themselves against an opponent with a prestigious soccer history. The United States easily won Group C, defeating Cuba, 3–0, and Costa Rica, 2–1. The United States, in an attack spearheaded by Preki and Wynalda, dominated their opponents with ease. The defense, held together by goalkeeper Kasey Keller and Pope, looked impenetrable; at least it did against mid-tier regional opponents. Brazil, runner-up in Group A to Jamaica, had managed only one victory—4–0 versus El Salvador—with a roster mostly made up of players younger than 23.

That set up a semifinal clash between the United States and Brazil on February 10, in Los Angeles. For all of Brazil's one-name wonders, it was an American player with a single name, Preki, who decided the match with a left-footed strike that won the United States the game and put them in the history books. After a career that included the Tacoma Stars of the MISL, Preki made a name for himself in MLS as an outdoor player with Kansas City. After gaining U.S. citizenship in 1996, he became part of the U.S. national team and continued to score goals. His 65th minute strike against Brazil was the biggest of the four goals he scored for the United States in 28 appearances. "I have scored a lot of goals in my life, but I will never forget that one," Preki said. "To come off the bench that night and score a goal was really wonderful. But I didn't do it alone. Kasey was the star. He made the saves and kept us in the game that night. He was great."

Preki's goal aside, the Americans would never have won the game without Keller in net. The goalkeeper made 10 saves to preserve the win. It may well have been the best performance by a goalie wearing the U.S. jersey. Keller played so well that the great Romario, during the course of the match, even shook Keller's hand following yet another wonderful save. Romario admitted afterward to reporters that Keller had put together the "greatest performance by a goalkeeper ever."

Making the win even greater was that the team was missing stalwarts Ramos, Reyna, and Dooley to injury. "We knew we were playing against an exceptional Brazil team, a team that had Romario, one of the greatest strikers in the history of the game," Sampson told USSoccer.com in 2013. "But on that day, it was all about Kasey Keller, his exceptional play, and how brilliant he was in that game. Romario calls it one of the best goalkeeper performances in the history of soccer, and I agree." Despite that amazing win, the United States went on to lose the Gold Cup final, 1–0, to Mexico, while Brazil finished third with a win against Jamaica.

1998 WORLD CUP

The 1998 World Cup, held in France, presented a big test for the United States. MLS was just two years old, not enough time to develop future talent. At the same time, the team had a core of veterans it could rely on. What had promised to be a tournament where the Americans hoped to

Photo 7.10.   Steve Sampson coached the U.S. at the 1998 World Cup in France. (Cal Poly)

be successful would turn out to be one remembered for being a fiasco. Drawn in Group F, with Germany, Yugoslavia, and Iran, the United States would disappoint. Germany placed first thanks to goal differential after finishing in a tie with Yugoslavia at seven points. The United States had never won a World Cup game on European soil at this point and kept that awful streak alive in France.

Under Sampson, the team had hoped to improve on the results achieved four years earlier at home. But Sampson made some drastic changes. He dropped Harkes from the roster (leaving everyone in the dark as to why) and benched such defensive mainstays as Balboa and Lalas. The reason for the Harkes decision, however, would be made public more than a decade later amid revelations that the then-captain had an "inappropriate relationship" with Wynalda's wife. Harkes denied that any such relationship, as described by Wynalda in February 2010 during the TV show *Fox Football Fone-in*, ever took place.

If the situation had become uneasy off the field, it also remained contentious on it. With MLS still in its infancy, Sampson could not solely rely on American-born players—something he would later blame his team's failings on. Sampson had also decided that the team would set up training camp and stay at the secluded Chateau de Pizay, in the isolated countryside just north of Lyon. The move to train in such seclusion was criticized by some players, particularly Lalas, and was counter to the excitement Milutinovic had generated by having his players bask in the thrill that was an event like the World Cup.

On the eve of the finals, Sampson put defender David Regis on the roster. Regis, who was born in France, had become a U.S. citizen just five weeks before the start of the World Cup. He became eligible for citizenship because his wife was American. Dooley, who had played for the United States in the 1994 World Cup, was back and had been named captain. Also on the team was Roy Wegerle, a native of South Africa, while Preki, who was born in Yugoslavia and became a U.S. citizen in 1996, after playing for nearly a decade in the MISL, also made the team.

The United States opened the tournament on June 15, against Germany, in front of 43,815 fans in Paris. The team was looking for at least a tie—and its first World Cup points on European soil—but the Germans had other plans. The Americans never had a chance, generating little offensively and playing too naïvely in the back. Germany walked all over Sampson's team, taking the lead after just eight minutes, with Andreas Möller, only to double the score with Jurgen Klinsmann in the 64th minute. Frankie Hejduk produced the only scoring chance for the Americans, nearly tying the game in the 52nd minute. Regis sent a cross to Hejduk, whose shot was headed just inside the right post. German goalkeeper Andreas Köpke dove to his right and made the save. Reyna followed up with a shot, but it bounced off Köpke's knees. The Germans' win propelled them to the top of the group standings.

The United States needed a victory against Iran to stave off elimination. Ironically, the Iranian team was coached by Jalal Talebi, who had lived in California for 17 years and taken over the team just two weeks prior to the start of the tournament. But the game also had political implications. The U.S. relationship with Iran had been strained by decades of conflict stemming from the Islamic Revolution of 1979. The game, however, was a chance to make amends.

The U.S. players, meanwhile, had bigger things on their minds. They needed a victory. Sampson was losing control of the team after Balboa and Lalas publicly stated that they were dissatisfied with sitting on the bench. The coach decided to change his formation against Iran, scrapping his 3–6–1 lineup used against Germany in favor of a 3–5–2, with Brian McBride and Wegerle on attack, and moving Hejduk to the midfield.

The United States played Iran on June 21, in Lyon, only days after U.S. president Bill Clinton called for improved relations with the Middle Eastern nation. The teams also heeded the call. The Iranian players shook hands with the Americans before kickoff, even handing them white flowers and posing together for a group photo. The pleasantries would end there. On the field, the Iranians outplayed the Americans, winning, 2–1, and knocking Sampson's team out of the tournament. A shot by Regis in the 68th minute hit the post, and a goal by Mehdi Mahdavikia past Keller in the 83rd minute sealed the win, the first for Iran at a World Cup. The

Americans would only score five minutes later, when McBride's header made its way into the back of the net.

Sampson, under pressure for losing against Germany, had no good excuse for the loss, even saying he would put the same lineup on the field against Yugoslavia despite criticism as to why he left Wynalda on the bench. Sampson had no answer. All that remained, it appeared, was to fire Sampson. U.S. Soccer did no such thing.

The U.S. team, which had lost two games and scored just one goal, had to play Yugoslavia in its last game. Four days after losing to Iran, they took on the Yugoslavs in a game they needed to win to salvage some pride. Sampson's team couldn't even do that in Nantes, although Hejduk, one of the few bright spots on the team, saw his header hit the post just 24 seconds into the contest. Three minutes later, Yugoslavia took the lead when Slobodan Komljenovic's header beat Brad Friedel off a rebound from Sinisa Mihajlovic's 35-yard free kick to make it 1–0. The goal proved to be the winner, even though the Americans had played well and created more chances.

The Americans finished the tournament 0–3, with goal differential ensuring it would finish last in the 32-nation field. Lalas didn't mince words when speaking about the failed expedition. He had told the *Washington Post*, on the eve of the Yugoslavia game, that Sampson's tactics had been all wrong:

> It's rather naive to think that a team that has gone through so much together can basically be rearranged and be expected to play with any consistency and cohesiveness. It just doesn't happen, especially in soccer. . . . The reality is, consistency comes from playing under a system for an extended period of time and understanding the role you play in that system. If this was the master plan, good god, it was pretty masterful. [Sampson's] got a weird definition of a master plan.

Sampson refused to respond to those complaints—saying only that he wished that those who were angered by his moves would keep their disapproval private. On June 29, four days after the U.S. elimination, the coach announced his resignation. The U.S. showing appeared to demonstrate to everyone that the country remained a lightweight when it came to international soccer. The program had reached its lowest point in years.

Sampson would be replaced with D.C. United coach Bruce Arena. His primary mission was to make sure the national team program was on track to qualify for the 2002 World Cup. Following the World Cup, U.S. Soccer created Project 2010, a program with a stated goal of winning the World Cup by 2010. The project's aim was also to recruit top youth players from throughout the country and give them a place to train and develop their skills. The project, fueled by $50 million in money from Nike, would have mixed results in the coming decade.

1999 FIFA CONFEDERATIONS CUP

In 1999, FIFA decided to host the Confederations Cup in Mexico, the first time soccer's world governing body had taken over what had been called the King Fahd Cup. The defending Gold Cup champion was Mexico, so the United States was also awarded a berth after finishing as runner-up at the tournament the previous year. The eight-team competition also featured such soccer heavyweights as Brazil and Germany. The United States was placed in Group B, with Brazil, Germany, and New Zealand, the tougher of the two in the first round. New coach Bruce Arena, who had garnered success in MLS with DC United, was tasked with guiding the United States into a new era.

The United States—still in rebuilding mode after the previous year's World Cup disaster—opened the tournament on July 24, at Estadío Jalisco, in Guadalajara, with a 2–1 victory against New Zealand. Goals by McBride and Jovan Kirovski clinched the win that day. Four days later, at the same venue, the United States lost to Brazil, 1–0, in a rematch of its 1998 Gold Cup game. Ronaldinho scored the game's only goal in the 13th minute. Needing only a draw against Germany in the final first-round match, the United States got the win, stunning Germany, 2–0, on July 30. Ben Olsen and Joe-Max Moore scored the goals in that game to lead the Americans to an improbable win.

"Before the tournament, I had three challenges for our team," Arena told reporters on the eve of the Germany game. "One, to get three points against New Zealand. Two, keep the result close against Brazil, so we can go into [the Germany game] with a fair chance for playing on Sunday. And three is now the key. It is a real exercise to get the appropriate result in this circumstance. The team is aware of the challenge. It will be a real good test of what we've learned."

Arena and his players were on a high. The victory, however, had set up a semifinal game against rival Mexico at Estadío Azteca in Mexico City, a traditionally treacherous venue for visiting teams. The national-team program was in a different place. The team looked up to the task—something that hadn't been the case a few years earlier before MLS. "The difference [in 1999] from five to seven years ago is that we have full-time professional players. On any given day they can compete with any team in the world," Arena told reporters on the eve of the match.

Played in front of 82,000 fans, the game ended scoreless after 90 minutes, pushing the match into overtime in the searing midday heat. Cuauhtemoc Blanco broke the deadlock, scoring what turned out to be the game-winner for Mexico seven minutes into extra time. The United States would go on to take third place, defeating Saudi Arabia, 2–0, in Guadalajara. Goals from Paul Bravo and McBride helped the United States equal its best finish—third place—at a FIFA tournament for the first time since the 1930 World Cup. Once again, Keller made the difference for the Americans. He was named to the tournament's All-Star Team, beating out Mexico's Jorge Campos and Brazil's Dida.

Arena had been able to turn the team around after the Sampson debacle with a series of impressive performances. "We earned everything we received in this tournament," Arena told reporters after the game. "It's been a great experience for these players to come into this tournament and perform as well as they did under some tough conditions." For the United States, the best was yet to come.

8

America's Team:
2000–2010

2000 CONCACAF GOLD CUP

The fifth edition of CONCACAF's premier tournament featured three invited teams from outside the region—Peru, Colombia, and South Korea. The 12-team field also featured favorites Mexico and the United States, both once again poised to contend for the crown. In the end, Canada would go on to shock the field, winning the Gold Cup in the final against Colombia.

The Americans were placed in Group B, with Peru and Haiti, a manageable group for Bruce Arena's men. The United States opened the group on February 12, with a 3–0 victory against Haiti at the Orange Bowl in Miami. Another win four days later at the same venue—a 1–0 result versus Peru—clinched the group and a berth to the knockout round, with Cobi Jones's strike after 59 minutes determining the outcome.

Winning Group B did nothing to give the Americans a favorable opponent. The United States was pitted against Colombia in the quarterfinals. The sides met on February 19, at the Orange Bowl, a venue teeming with Colombia fans. What the 33,000 spectators in attendance witnessed was a rollicking 2–2 game after 120 minutes that needed a penalty shootout to get a winner. The Americans had twice taken the lead in regulation—1–0 on a goal from Eric Wynalda in the 20th minute and 2–1 thanks to Chris Armas in the 51st. The Americans squandered both leads as Colombia put on a strong offensive display in the second half. Hampering U.S. efforts was an injury to Brian McBride, which forced him to leave the match. In the shootout, Colombia got the better of the

United States, 2–1, after the Americans failed to score with Wynalda, Reyna, Armas, and Ben Olsen.

In an interview with *Soccer America*, Arena said the tournament never gave his team a real chance to "size ourselves up" against strong CONCACAF opponents. "In terms of the competition, I was very pleased to have the opportunity to play Peru and Colombia, but at the end of the day I learn nothing about our team in terms of where we stand in CONCACAF. That, to me, is disappointing," he said.

2002 CONCACAF GOLD CUP

After a disappointing finish in 2000, the United States hoped to make a splash at the Gold Cup in the lead-up to the World Cup in Korea/Japan. In 2001, the team achieved its fourth straight World Cup qualification. MLS grew into a key contributor to the overall quality of the national team player pool. Project 40 had 18 MLS-based players. Landon Donovan, at this point, had blossomed into a strong player, both in MLS and for the national team. Paul Caligiuri announced his retirement in 2001, ending one era for the national team, but 2002 opened a new one.

The 2002 Gold Cup featured 12 teams—the Americans placed in Group B, with Cuba and South Korea, invited as a special guest. Arena knew this was the time for his side to have a breakout year. A 2–1 victory against the South Koreans on January 18, at the Rose Bowl in Pasadena, and a narrow 1–0 defeat of Cuba two days later put the Americans in the knockout stage. In the quarterfinals, the Americans were pitted against El Salvador. This was a potentially tricky encounter given how Central American teams had often found a way to defeat the United States, but Arena's men clobbered their opponents, 4–0, in front of 32,000 at the Rose Bowl. McBride shined with a hat trick in the span of the first 21 minutes. In the semifinals on January 30, against Canada, it would take a penalty shootout to decide a winner after a scoreless draw. A mere 7,241 fans watched the Americans win, 4–2, in the shootout.

The United States won its second Gold Cup on February 2, defeating Costa Rica, 2–0, playing in front of 14,432 onlookers at the Rose Bowl. A strong defensive effort allowed the Americans to thwart any Costa Rican attempt, while the midfield clicked, allowing the United States to take the lead in the 37th minute with Josh Wolff, who outraced the Costa Rican defense to get on the end of a great ball out of the back from defender Frankie Hejduk. Wolff held off his marker and slotted his shot home from the top of the penalty area with his left foot, tucking it inside the right post past Costa Rican goalkeeper Erick Lonnis. "I've had my difficulties in the tournament . . . but that's life as a forward," Wolff told reporters at the postgame news conference. "You have to stick with it and know that if you're getting your chances you're doing something right. To be able to stick one in certainly gives me a lot of confidence."

The Americans made it 2–0 in the 63rd minute, when defender Jeff Agoos hit a superb 25-yard free kick from the top of the penalty box, spinning the ball and perfectly placing it into the right side past Lonnis. "We faced a lot of criticism [in 2001], maybe some deserved; most unwarranted," Arena told reporters after the match. "Even in the beginning of this tournament, we took a lot of criticism. For the guys to work hard and be deserving of this cup is very special for both the players and the coaching staff."

2002 WORLD CUP QUALIFYING

Arena's team would finish second in the Hexagonal (tied with Mexico), behind Costa Rica, to earn a place in the World Cup. The highlight of qualification was the home match against Mexico. On February 28, 2001, the United States made history in the shape of a 2–0 victory against its regional rivals. Aside from the win, the Americans made a statement that evening in Columbus, Ohio. After decades of failing to harness any home-field advantage, U.S. Soccer finally figured out a way to gain an edge.

Officials scheduled the U.S.–Mexico match at Columbus Crew Stadium, the thought-process being that a cold Midwestern city was just the thing Mexico could not withstand. They were correct. The Mexican players remained in their locker room rather than warm up before the game. "I remember the look on their faces when they lined up for the national anthems. They looked cold," recalled Agoos. "I knew then it would be a tough game for them." With the temperature at 29 degrees—and a wind chill factor that made it feel like it was in the teens—the game was dubbed "La Guerra Fria," Spanish for "The Cold War."

The cold was the least of Mexico's problems that evening. With the pro-U.S. crowd behind it (a sellout of 25,000 fans), the team took it to Mexico. The difference-maker was an injury to McBride. After suffering a severe cut on his forehead—a result of a hard crash with defender Rafael Marquez—that caused him to have a swollen right eye, McBride was done after just 15 minutes. Arena decided to sub in Wolff. If that wasn't enough, Reyna was forced out of the match in the 43rd minute with a left groin strain. He was replaced by midfielder Clint Mathis. Both Wolff and Mathis would make a difference. Just two minutes into the second half, Mathis played a long ball from the back to Wolff. He aptly used his speed to latch onto the ball and then slid it past a charging Jorge Campos for the 1–0 lead. Wolff then created the second goal, pushing defender Alberto

Marcias to the endline and drawing Campos out, laying a pass across the penalty box. Earnie Stewart met the pass and made it 2–0 in the 87th minute.

Wolff and Mathis were exactly the type of players the national team was hoping MLS would spawn. Drafted by the Chicago Fire in 1998, Wolff set the record for goals by a rookie in MLS by tallying eight times in 14 games. He quickly became one of Arena's go-to strikers. Mathis, who had joined the league the same year, played with the Los Angeles Galaxy. In 2000, he was dealt to the New York/New Jersey MetroStars, scoring 33 goals in 67 games from 2000 to 2003. Known for his ability to score with both his head and feet, Mathis became one of the league's best strikers.

The Americans would go on to defeat Mexico, 2–0, and the game would forever be referred to as "Dos a Cero." It would also be the first of a series of 2–0 wins against Mexico. "That was obviously a great win for the U.S. team. We really wanted to get three points against a very fine Mexican team, and we did that," Arena said in the postgame news conference. "We faced a lot of adversity in the first half and had to make a couple of changes. I'm proud of the way the team pulled together at halftime, went out, and did the job in the second half to get the victory."

The team Arena had assembled had been built primarily on the shoulders of the U.S. Under-17 roster that finished fourth at the 1999 U-17 World Championship in New Zealand. The team, coached by John Ellinger, featured Donovan, who won the tournament MVP award, and midfielder DaMarcus Beasley, as well as defenders Oguchi Onyewu and Kyle Beckerman. At a time when U.S. Soccer was basking in the glory of having a women's team win the World Cup at home, it was equally important to again field a competitive men's team. The foundation was put in place; the results would eventually come in the form of World Cup success.

2002 WORLD CUP

The tournament—cohosted by South Korea and Japan—marked the first time the World Cup would be played in Asia. Although the usual nations, such as Germany and Brazil, were favorites to win it all, it would be a tournament highlighted by Cinderella teams. One of those teams would turn out to be the United States. Placed in Group D, the Americans had to face Portugal, Poland, and South Korea. It was not an easy group, but Arena was up for the challenge. His 23-player roster featured 12 men from MLS teams and another 11 who played professionally in Europe. Mathis led the group of players based in MLS. He had gone on a scoring tear for the national team going into the World Cup, compiling an amazing eight goals and six assists in just 19 games. The team convened in Cary, North Carolina, for 10 days of training before playing three friendlies to prepare for the tournament.

Once in South Korea, the squad wasted little time making an impact. On June 5, the United States defeated Portugal, 3–2, at Suwon Stadium in Suwon. The Americans took the lead after just four minutes, with John O'Brien, after goalkeeper Vitor Baia failed to clear a McBride header. The ball fell to O'Brien, who was standing just a few yards from the Portuguese goal and buried it in the back of the net. The United States served up a one–two punch in the 29th minute, when a Donovan cross was deflected off defender Jorge Costa for the unfortunate own goal. The Americans led, 2–0, and were in total control of the match. They made it 3–0 when defender Tony Sanneh executed a perfect cross into the box for McBride with nine minutes left in the half. He put the ball past Baia with a diving header near the far post. Sanneh and McBride, who had once been teammates with the A-League's Milwaukee Rampage, put together a play that would highlight the U.S. win. "The important thing was to come out quick," said McBride. "They're a very good team, and we needed to make sure and put them on their heels, and that's what we did."

The Portuguese ended the first half on a positive note. In the 39th minute, off a corner kick, O'Brien's clearance fell to the feet of Beto, who put the ball past goalkeeper Brad Friedel for the goal. Portugal pressured the U.S. defense in the second half, forcing the Americans to lock themselves down in their own half. Nonetheless, Portugal was able to get a goal in the 71st minute, but only after Jeff Agoos put the ball into his own net. Unable to gain possession, the Americans were forced to soak up the pressure in the final stretch of the game. They were able to successfully let the clock run out to record one of the biggest upsets in tournament history. Afterward, Arena told reporters at a news conference that the victory was "probably the biggest win in the modern era" for American soccer. "We came into this game believing we could win this game, and our guys played a great 30 to 40 minutes in the first half that really won the game for us," he added.

A win against South Korea in their next game would put the Americans through to the second round for the first time since 1994. On June 10, the United States squared off against South Korea in Daegu. The Americans picked up where they left off against Portugal, playing aggressively and moving the ball forward in the hopes of taking the lead. Arena's offensive-minded strategy paid off in the end. In the 24th minute, O'Brien's long pass from midfield found striker Clint Mathis near the edge of the South Korean box. Mathis unleashed a left-footed shot into the lower-left corner of the net for the lead. The South Koreans had their chance to tie the match when Agoos pulled down Hwang Sun-Hong in the penalty box.

Friedel's spectacular save denied Lee Eul-Yong from the penalty spot. Kim Nam-Il's follow-up attempt off a rebound went wide of the left post.

The South Koreans applied more pressure in the second half despite Friedel's ability to save everything in his path. But South Korea, backed by an energetic home crowd, got the equalizer with 12 minutes left to play, when Lee Eul-Yong served up a free kick from midfield into the box, where striker Ahn Jung-Hwan was able to outjump the U.S. defense and head the ball past Friedel. The ensuing goal celebration featured the players mimicking the moves of a speed skater, a reference to their countryman who had been disqualified during the Winter Olympics earlier in the year, giving the United States a gold medal. The game ended, 1–1. "It was a difficult game, but I am happy with the point," Arena told reporters. "Korea's fitness is outstanding. Most people, a month ago, would not have believed the United States would get four points in our first two matches."

The Americans were on the verge of reaching the knockout round. The U.S. team had to defeat Poland in its final match or hope for a Portugal loss against South Korea. While the United States would lose to Poland, 3–1, in Daejeon, South Korea would pull off the upset—one of many at the tournament—with its 1–0 victory against Portugal. The Americans had backed into the knockout round and would finish second in the group to South Korea. "Nobody would have picked out the results in this group," Arena said. "It was an unusual World Cup. There will be interesting results ahead of us."

Next up for the Americans was a meeting with Mexico on June 17, in Jeonju. The all-CONCACAF matchup was expected to be thrilling given the bad blood that had developed between the neighboring countries throughout the years. The Mexicans wasted little time applying pressure on the American backline, but the United States took the lead. Against the run of play, Reyna ran the ball down the right flank and crossed it to striker Josh Wolff. His crisp pass to McBride gave him just enough space to release a wicked shot that beat goalkeeper Oscar Perez for the lead after eight minutes. The Mexicans dominated possession for long stretches of the first half and wasted several chances. With Friedel having another top-notch performance in net, the first half ended with the United States ahead, 1–0. The Americans played tough defensively, using the counterattack to their advantage. Once again, the United States scored against the run of play in the 65th minute, when a cross from Eddie Lewis found Donovan inserted near the far post. Donovan coolly headed the ball past Perez for the 2–0 lead to seal the win. Once again, it was a 2–0 win for the United States versus Mexico. The victorious Americans had reached the quarterfinals, shocking the soccer world in the process. "There has been a lot of bad blood over the years [against Mexico]," Arena said at a news conference after the game, "but when the game is over, we're friends again. Mexico is a great team, and I'm proud of my guys. It is a great day for U.S. soccer."

Nonetheless, Arena had his critics. Those uncomfortable with a team like the United States challenging the planet's established soccer powers labeled the squad lucky. Arena, always composed, didn't let the skeptics get to him. He knew the United States outclassed Portugal in the first round and had now successfully eliminated Mexico. "I don't know if we were lucky. We beat the winner of the group with Italy," Arena told reporters, referring to Mexico.

In the United States, soccer fever was growing despite games being broadcast at 2 a.m. For the first time in decades, the United States looked like a World Cup contender, trying to reach the semifinals for the first time since 1930. To achieve such a feat, the Americans had to overcome Germany in Ulsan. Arena knew defeating Germany would not be easy, but after overcoming Mexico, the team was confident a victory was not impossible. Another upset could happen—and almost did on June 21. The victory against Mexico had landed Donovan on the cover of *Sports Illustrated*, relegating the Los Angeles Lakers and Detroit Red Wings— winners of the NBA championship and Stanley Cup, respectively—to the inside pages.

The Americans quickly put Germany on its heels. In the 17th minute, a dazzling solo run by Donovan down the right side ended with a curling shot that was tipped away by Oliver Kahn. Thirteen minutes later, Donovan once again scampered down the field, beating the German offside trap after a pass from Reyna, but Kahn was there once again to block the shot. While the Germans threatened from set pieces, it was the Americans who came close to scoring again. McBride broke down the left flank in the 36th minute, feeding a pass to Lewis, whose shot was too weak, and Kahn made the save. Germany, for its part, did not give up. Against the run of play, Michael Ballack headed the ball past Friedel in the 39th minute off a corner kick by Christian Ziege from the right side for the 1–0 lead at the half.

The Americans did get the ball over the line in the 50th minute, but Scottish referee Hugh Dallas made a bad call. Even though defender Gregg Berhalter's shot had crossed the line, unleashing cheers among the 38,000 fans inside Munsu Stadium, it was then deflected by Kahn, ricocheting off the forearm of German defender Torsten Frings and back toward the German goalkeeper. Berhalter looked at the referee, thinking it was a handball, which, if called by Dallas, would have resulted in a penalty kick. The call never came, although some of the players argued it should have been a goal because the ball had initially crossed the line. TV replays supported the argument. The Americans tried everything to get a goal, but the German defense was too tough to beat.

Photo 8.1.   Cobi Jones in action at the 2002 World Cup against Poland. (John Todd/ ISI Photos)

The game proved entertaining in the second half but unproductive for the U.S. players. It wasn't until the final minute that a Mathis cross from the right was headed by Sanneh toward Kahn, but the ball hit the side netting. The Americans had not been lucky. In fact, this team had been unlucky to lose, 1–0. Germany may have gotten the win, but the crowd cheered for the Americans. "We were pretty confident that we could pressure them and create some chances," Arena said during a press conference. "I think we did that. The difference in the game, besides the goal by Ballack, was Kahn. He came up with some great saves and kept them in the match in the early going, and he came up with some saves in the second half that kept us off the board."

McBride said the 2002 tournament remains one of his most indelible memories. "On and off the field, it was a great time for me, my teammates, and our families," he said. "Personally, it was very satisfying. To score goals against Portugal and Mexico were both equally amazing. We really worked for each other on that team, and I think the results showed that."

2005 CONCACAF GOLD CUP

In 2004, the national team held its first January camp, a chance for MLS players to convene at the Home Depot Center (now StubHub Center) to train and play a friendly. Arena called in 27 players for a three-week training period that culminated with a 1–1 draw on January 18, against Denmark. Donovan scored a penalty-kick goal in the 77th minute to level the score. The official start to the 2006 World Cup cycle had begun. The January camp is held to this day and continues to be the place for the team to remain sharp.

In 2005, the United States successfully defended its title as the Gold Cup grew in both popularity and stature. The tournament took place in the midst of qualifying for the 2006 World Cup, allowing the United States to test some players and gain valuable experience. The competition also featured two guest teams: South Africa and Colombia. The Americans were placed in Group B, with Costa Rica, Canada, and Cuba. The team won its first two games (4–1 against Cuba and 2–0 versus Canada). The United States ended the group stage undefeated after a scoreless draw against Costa Rica.

In the quarterfinals, the United States defeated Jamaica, 3–1, at Gillette Stadium in Foxboro, Massachusetts. Wolff opened the scoring and Beasley added two more to grab the win. Beasley, a Project-40 player, had played in MLS with the Galaxy and Chicago Fire but moved to Dutch club

PSV Eindoven in 2004. Part of a growing number of Americans signing with European teams, he was a versatile player, able to play in the middle as a midfielder and on either wing. His ball distribution skills and ability to find open players in the penalty box made him an offensive threat.

Next up was Honduras in the semifinals. The Americans won, 2–1, a come-from-behind effort at Giants Stadium in East Rutherford, New Jersey, in front of 41,721 fans. The United States, without Arena, who had been ejected after arguing a call midway through the second half, tied the match four minutes from the end via John O'Brien's close-range strike. Two minutes into stoppage time, Oguchi Onyewu scored his first U.S. goal off a diving header that hit the underside of the crossbar.

The Americans faced Panama, the tournament's Cinderella team, on July 24, at Giants Stadium. What should have been a manageable opponent turned into a difficult 120 minutes. The game had failed to produce a goal, and the 31,000 in attendance watched the game go to a shootout. An outstanding day from Kasey Keller in goal allowed the United States to defend its title, downing Panama, 3–1. Keller saved Panama's first shot and also got help from the crossbar and a badly taken kick that sailed high over the bar. Santino Quaranta and Landon Donovan scored their attempts, with Brad Davis tallying the deciding shot. "Every single game in this tournament Kasey Keller made a big play for us. He has shown his quality the whole time," assistant coach Glenn Myernick, on the bench for the suspended Arena, told reporters. "In the end of it, both teams were fatigued, and, fortunately, we were able to come out ahead."

2006 WORLD CUP QUALIFYING

The United States won the Hexagonal, edging out Mexico on goal differential for the top spot. It was the first time since 1934 that the Americans had become the first team to qualify out of its region. Arena's success continued as the U.S. team solidly positioned itself, alongside Mexico, as the strongest squad in the region. Speaking of World Cup qualifying, Arena said the following in a conference call with reporters:

> Our stature has improved since '98. Anytime we play these types of games they're going to be difficult. I don't perceive us to be a giant. This time around, I think our players remember the qualifying process from 2000 and 2001, and how difficult it was and the highs and lows and the things we went through to make us a team, we're well aware of that. We also left the 2002 World Cup with a real good feeling. I think that motivates our group. I think we want to get back to the World Cup and place ourselves in a position to do well again, and we know it's a long road to get there. The whole process

is exciting to the group. The only expectations we have our within our team. There is no pressure from the outside, the pressure is internal.

The United States, struggling to get points on the road against Mexico, continued to get the best of its rivals when hosting them. The United States again posted a *dos a cero* against Mexico in Columbus. This time, the victory allowed the Americans to clinch a spot in Germany in 2006. The September 3, 2005, match featured all the trappings of that 2001 qualifier. Although not as cold, the teams tangled with one another, a physical contest that players like Onyewu, the towering U.S. defender, relished. Jared Borgetti was stopped by Onyewu nearly every time the Mexican striker got the ball. It made for an easy night in goal for Keller.

The sellout crowd went into ecstasy when the United States took the lead after 53 minutes. The goal was a team effort and a thing of beauty. An Eddie Lewis free kick found Onyewu's head. The defender headed the ball, only to be stopped by the left post. But the ball bounced across the goal line, allowing Steve Ralston to bang it in with a close-range header past goalkeeper Oswaldo Sanchez. Up 1–0, the Americans grew even more confident than they had been in the first half. They were able to successfully stretch the Mexican backline and doubled the lead five minutes later off a corner kick. Reyna's pass allowed Beasley to slot the ball into the net with a curling left-footed shot. History had repeated itself, 2–0. "It always means a lot to beat Mexico," Keller told reporters after the game. "To beat Mexico to qualify and to finish this thing off and to beat them comfortably, 2–0, is even better. It just makes it better."

2006 WORLD CUP

The United States entered the World Cup with a renewed energy and focus that it could win big games. The experiences of four years earlier had clearly sent a message that Arena was the man able to get the most from this group. What the Americans lacked was that star player who could get them far in a tournament such as the World Cup. Making matters worse, arguably the most talented American not on the national-team roster was Giuseppe Rossi. While Freddy Adu had been widely hailed as the future of American soccer—he would end up only making 12 appearances for the United States and never at a World Cup—it was the New Jersey-born Rossi who had burst onto the scene as that standout star U.S. fans had always dreamed about. Rossi, however, held dual citizenship, and it was his parents' Italian birth that allowed him to move to Parma at age 12, to play and train in the club's youth system.

When he turned 17 in 2004, Rossi transferred to Manchester United and made his pro debut with the English giants, although he was a reserve. Between 2004 and 2007, he played in just five Premier League games. Although Rossi had represented Italy at the youth level, Arena invited him to train with the United States in 2006, ahead of the World Cup. But Rossi declined, telling Arena he wished to play for Italy. Arena told reporters at the time, "We're not chasing around 18-year-old players that can't get games for their club team and tell me they want to play for Italy."

In 2009, Fernando Rossi, Giuseppe's father, told the *New York Times*, "Giuseppe took a big chance that he would make the Italian team. It was his goal. He was born [in America], but he grew up soccer-wise in that environment." The gamble never really paid off for Rossi. Although he has represented Italy 30 times at the senior level, Rossi has never played in a World Cup.

With Rossi not a factor, Arena focused on the players he did have. The coach exuded confidence that the United States could muster a repeat performance of 2006; however, returning to Europe—the 2006 World Cup was to be played in Germany—also conjured up bad memories from the 1998 tournament in France. Despite the optimism, the reality was the Americans were to "have our hands full," as Arena put it, after the team was drawn into Group E, alongside Italy, Ghana, and the Czech Republic. "We'll decide on the field how difficult this group is," Arena told reporters.

What would be decided on the field highlighted the need for the United States to keep improving if it wanted to compete with the world's best teams. On June 12, the Czech Republic got the better of the United States, beating them, 3–0. The Czech Republic struck early when towering forward Jan Koller scored on a fifth-minute header. "Obviously, the first goal was big," Arena told reporters after the game. "To give that up in the first five minutes of the match really put us behind and allowed the Czech team to sit back and really counter at us." Counter the Czechs did. Tomas Rosicky added a 35-yard shot before the end of the half and scored a second on a breakaway late in the game.

The June 17 game versus Italy could have sealed the fate of the Americans—lose and go home, salvage a draw, and try to stay alive. What resulted was a 1–1 draw and one of the all-time greatest performances by the U.S. national squad. The outcome kept the Americans' hopes of advancing intact, while also showing off the team's grittiness and attitude.

The Italians took the lead after 22 minutes on a play that started when American Pablo Mastroeni fouled Francesco Totti 30 yards from goal. Andrea Pirlo's free kick floated the ball into the box, allowing Alberto Gilardino to head the ball into the net. Eddie Pope raised his arm trying

Photo 8.2. Brian McBride (left) after being elbowed in the face by Italy's Daniele De Rossi at the 2006 World Cup. (Chris Putman/ISI Photos)

to get the referee to whistle the Italian offside, but he was not. The Americans equalized five minutes later when a Bobby Convey free kick from the right sideline was misplayed by defender Cristian Zaccardo at the back post and went in for an own goal. The United States had caught a break.

A minute later, the United States found itself up a man when Daniele De Rossi was given a red card after elbowing McBride in the face. McBride briefly left the game with a cut under his left eye. Just before halftime, Mastroeni was shown a red card after a two-footed challenge brought down Pirlo. At the start of the second half, the United States would lose another player when Pope's foul on Gilardino from behind earned him his second yellow card of the night. Down to nine players, the American backline thwarted every chance the Italians could put together. "They've given everything. It would have been a shame to concede a goal late, but we stuck in this thing," Keller told reporters after the game. "We're in this tournament, and we have a good chance now. Of course, we wanted three points, but the point in these circumstances is phenomenal."

The Americans needed a win on June 22, against Ghana, to advance out of the first round. A 2–1 loss, however, dashed those hopes. Like the Italy match, the Americans played a physical game in hopes of intimidating their opponents. With both Mastroeni and Pope out due to suspension, Arena knew the task would be even more difficult without his two best players in the lineup. In the 22nd minute, Ghana scored when Reyna turned the ball over in his own half, allowing Haminu Draman to score on Keller. Reyna, who suffered a sprained MCL on the play, was taken off on a stretcher. He returned in the 27th minute but only lasted 13 more minutes before he was replaced by Ben Olsen.

The United States mounted a comeback. In the 43rd minute, DaMarcus Beasley beat out three Ghana players and sent a cross that Clint Dempsey buried with a one-timer. The game would be settled in first-half stoppage time when referee Markus Merk called a penalty, deeming Oguchi Onyewu's challenge on Razak Pimpong at the top of the penalty box too rough. In fact, the header was clean, but Pimpong collapsed to the ground in dramatic fashion to get the call. Stephen Appiah scored the penalty kick to win the game. "We're disappointed with the decision of the referee, but at the end of it we didn't make the plays that we needed to make," Keller told reporters. "It's as simple as that." It would be another World Cup of missed opportunities for the United States.

2007 CONCACAF GOLD CUP

The national team used the 2007 Gold Cup to assert its domination of the region—and of Mexico—thanks to a string of strong performances at the tournament. The United States swept aside its Group B opponents in easy fashion, defeating Guatemala (1–0), Trinidad and Tobago (2–0), and El Salvador (4–0). In the quarterfinals, the Americans faced Panama on June 16, in Foxboro, a rematch of the 2005 championship game. Goals from Donovan on a penalty kick in the 60th minute and a Carlos Bocanegra tally two minutes later led to a 2–1 victory. For new coach Bob Bradley, it was a major victory after he had been given the national-team reins on a full-time basis in the spring after serving as interim manager following Arena's exit after the World Cup.

A native of New Jersey and graduate of Princeton, Bradley had been Arena's assistant at DC United during the early MLS years. He coached the Chicago Fire to the MLS Cup and U.S. Open Cup titles in 1998, the team's expansion year. Although many had speculated that Bradley had been poised to get the national-team job, U.S. Soccer had tried to get former German international Jurgen Klinsmann to take the position. But negotiations with Klinsmann, who lived in California, fell through—and Bradley was officially given the job in December 2006.

On June 21, the United States played Canada in the semifinals at Chicago's Soldier Field in front of a crowd of 60,000. In perhaps one of the most controversial finishes in team history, the Americans won, 2–1. Frankie Hejduk put the United States ahead in the 39th minute, and Donovan's penalty kick put the team up, 2–0, at halftime. Canada scored in the 76th minute, putting its attack into hyper-drive in an effort to earn a draw. With Keller on his toes, the Americans found themselves down a man when Michael Bradley was red-carded following a tackle on Julian De Guzman. Up a man, Canada looked to tie the match in the fourth minute of stoppage time, but Atiba Hutchinson's goal was ruled offside. It was a contentious decision. The Canadians protested in vain, and the United States escaped with the win.

The United States continued its domination of Mexico in the Gold Cup final, overcoming its rivals with a 2–1 come-from-behind win. The game, played on June 24, in front of a sellout crowd of 60,000 at Soldier Field, was one of the team's best efforts of the year. Spearheading the attack, Donovan helped erase an early 1–0 Mexico lead. Goals by Donovan and Benny Feilhaber in the second half propelled the team to victory. It would be the first in a string of many contests throughout the next few years where the Americans would win or salvage a draw after falling behind. The title also helped the United States qualify for the 2009 FIFA Confederations Cup.

Mexico took the lead right before halftime, with Jose Andres Guardado. After a locker room pep talk from Bradley and a tactical move that included replacing Pablo Mastroeni with Ricardo Clark, the Americans entered the second half energized. The United States tied the score following a team effort. The Americans seamlessly moved the ball, with

Jonathan Spector crossing the ball into the penalty box to Brian Ching. His attempt muffed when Jonny Magallon clipped Ching from behind, earning a penalty call. Donovan scored on the ensuing kick, the strike tying him with Wynalda for the all-time goal scoring lead.

The game tied, the United States continued to build up play from the back. Accurate passing and astute dead-ball play led to the second goal. A Donovan corner kick in the 72nd minute floated into the penalty area, cleared by the Mexican defense. But Feilhaber, well positioned at the top of the box, hit a one-time volley that blasted past the defense and a helpless Oswaldo Sanchez to win the match. "The first thing I was thinking of when the ball was coming in the air was that I'd had a couple of shots in the El Salvador game that were the same as that one," Feilhaber told reporters. "I was just looking to get good contact on the ball and send it toward the goal. I knew as soon as I hit it that it was going in. It felt great."

The United States did not stop there, with Ching hitting the right post on one occasion in the 76th minute. Another attempt slammed the woodwork in the 89th minute when Beasley's empty-net shot hit the crossbar. At the other end, Tim Howard made a key save near the end of the game to preserve the U.S. win. The victory allowed the Americans to finish the tournament with a perfect 6–0, outscoring opponents 13–3.

Howard was another in a long line of successful American-born goalkeepers. He also hailed from northern New Jersey, the same hotbed of soccer that had given the national team such players as Meola and Harkes more than a decade earlier. Howard began his pro career in MLS with the MetroStars but signed with Manchester United in England in 2003. He would go on to play 13 years in the English Premier League—signing with Everton in 2007—before returning to MLS in 2016, with the Colorado Rapids.

2007 COPA AMERICA

In 2007, the United States was invited to participate in the Copa America, played in Venezuela. Bradley's men were placed in a tough first-round group with Argentina, Paraguay, and Colombia. The team featured only nine players who had played in the Gold Cup. The roster, missing stars such as Donovan, who returned to MLS duty, was also heavy on youth, with 16 players having amassed 10 caps or less. One such player, defender Jay DeMerit, who only had three caps for the national team going into the tournament, reached soccer's big top in the most unlikely way.

DeMerit had also played baseball and run track during his high school days in Wisconsin, but it was soccer that he was most interested in. Although he played with Chicago Fire Premier, the development team of the Chicago Fire, DeMerit was not drafted or signed by any MLS teams. After working as a bartender, he took advantage of his European Union work status (due to his Danish grandfather) by moving to England in 2003, with only $1,800 in his pocket, in an attempt to find a club. It was an unusual journey and an atypical way of breaking into the game. He started off playing in the ninth-tier level with Southall. In 2004, DeMerit joined Northwood, a seventh-tier side, to play in some of their preseason matches. Northwood played Watford, a first-division club at the time. During the course of that game, DeMerit impressed then-Watford manager Ray Lewington enough to earn a two-week trial. DeMerit would sign a one-year contract with Watford to play in their 2004–2005 season. On May 21, 2006, in the playoff final against Leeds United, DeMerit reached the pinnacle of the sport—heading in the game's first goal as Watford gained promotion to the Premier League by defeating Leeds United, 3–0.

Meanwhile, for Bradley, the tournament was a chance to further mold the roster and assess talent. "Playing two major tournaments back-to-back is both a privilege and a difficult challenge in terms of putting together rosters, and this is something we've known all along," he told reporters on the eve of Copa America. "This group has many of the faces that could play a role in 2008 and 2009, when our focus turns to our ultimate goal of qualifying for the 2010 World Cup in South Africa."

With the Gold Cup title in the rearview mirror, the Americans were in the tournament to gain some experience. What it got in addition to that were sound defeats by top-class opponents. The United States went 0–3, losing to Argentina (4–1), Paraguay (3–1), and Colombia (1–0), to finish at the bottom of Group C. Despite the bad showing, Bradley was pleased with the experience his players had received and hoped the team could build on it heading into the Confederations Cup and 2010 World Cup.

Bradley's strategy was to create a larger talent pool—from players in MLS and those playing abroad—from which he could call up players. In an interview with the *New York Times*, he said, "We knew at the start of the summer that it was going to be a unique challenge to immediately switch gears and go from the Gold Cup to the Copa. We all understood the challenges, and we still feel like we gained experience."

2009 FIFA CONFEDERATIONS CUP

The Confederations Cup was a perfect opportunity for the United States to make a World Cup dry run a year ahead of the tournament. Setting up camp in South Africa and having the players acclimate to the weather and altitude of some of the venues would be key to Bradley's preparation. But the Confederations Cup would turn out to be more than a chance to have players get used to their surroundings; it would turn into an opportunity to showcase to the world how far U.S. soccer had come in just a decade.

The United States opened the Confederations Cup with a 3–1 loss to Italy and a 3–0 defeat by Brazil. Despite being 0–2, the Americans still had a shot at qualifying for the knockout round if they defeated Egypt by a margin of at least three goals and with a Brazil victory versus Italy by at least the same number of goals. The odds seemed insurmountable—U.S. Soccer's website called them "slim" on the eve of the game—but not with the group Bradley had put together.

On June 21, which also happened to be Father's Day, the United States took on Egypt, the African champions, at Royal Bafokeng Stadium in Rustenburg. Bradley's team dominated Egypt throughout the contest, putting together a 3–0 win with goals from Charlie Davies, Michael Bradley, and Clint Dempsey. Davies's goal came following a scramble in front of the net near the left post, after 21 minutes. While Brazil was dominating Italy in Pretoria, the Americans held on to a 1–0 lead at the half. Michael Bradley got the Americans—and his proud dad on the sidelines—a goal closer to the semis in the 63rd minute after a nice combination with Donovan. With the United States in need of a third goal, Bob Bradley took out Jozy Altidore and moved Dempsey higher up the field. The move worked, and a Dempsey header from a perfectly placed cross on the right flank from Jonathan Spector in the 71st minute completed the improbable win. Coupled with Italy's loss by the same score to Brazil, the Americans had the unlikely fortune of reaching the semifinals.

The next opponent for the United States was to be Spain, the defending European champions. It would be another uphill battle for Bradley's men—and yet another game in which pundits and fans alike would remain shocked at what would transpire. After the Egypt game, Dempsey told reporters, "The odds were against us, and the chances of us going through were slim. All we could control was ourselves. It's a credit to all the guys and the coaching staff. We worked hard this whole tournament so far and believed in ourselves. Now it's time to refocus and get ready for Spain."

The heroics the Americans had put together versus Egypt would be replicated on June 24, in Bloemfontein. The 2–0 U.S. victory remains one of the team's greatest upsets. It was another win that made the world sit up and take notice that Americans playing soccer well was a real thing, something that had been decades in the making. This game should have been, to put it mildly, a mismatch. Spain was one of the favorites to win the Confederations Cup. Winner of the European Championship the prior year, Spain had been on a winning tear. The team had finally lived up to its hype, and many were already picking them to win the 2010 World Cup—a feat it would accomplish a year later. Against the United States,

Spain was putting its 35-game undefeated streak on the line. By the time the match was over, the United States had stunned its opponent and the world. Goals by Altidore and Dempsey sealed the win and gave the top-ranked team on the planet its first defeat since November 2006.

The Americans did everything right that night at Free State Stadium, while Spain could not break through against goalkeeper Tim Howard and the tight U.S. defense. The Americans had finally come together after three weeks of training and games. "Whenever you beat a team that's ranked number one in the world it is a big deal," said defender Carlos Bocanegra. "To defeat Spain was great."

The U.S. backline that evening featured Bocanegra, making his first start at left back since March 2007, playing alongside Jay DeMerit, Oguchi Onyewu, and Jonathan Spector. With the American defense on lockdown, the United States nearly scored early on when a Davies bicycle kick off a Dempsey cross went just wide of the goal in the seventh minute. A minute later, another Davies shot went wide of goalkeeper Iker Casillas's goal, another message to Spain that the Americans had come to play.

At the other end, Spain, playing with the attacking trio of Fernando Torres, David Villa, and Cesc Fabregas, was unable to penetrate the U.S. defense. The game, played at a frenetic pace despite the chilly temperatures, staying below 55 degrees, featured a series of attempts on both sides, but the Americans were the ones to score. It was Altidore in the 27th minute who ended Spain's shutout streak at 451 minutes. Dempsey played a one–two with Davies and looked for Altidore, who was being marked by his Villareal teammate, Joan Capdevila. Dempsey's pass was deflected by Xabi Alonso, but Altidore was able to shoot the ball, which bounced off the hand of Casillas and into the net for the 1–0 lead. Altidore called scoring the goal "one of the biggest moments of his life."

With the Americans hanging on to preserve the lead, Spain upped the pressure in the second half. Howard made a series of saves to keep the Spanish off the scoreboard. In the 79th minute, the Americans put the game away when Dempsey made it 2–0. Spain seemed unmotivated at that point, a two-goal deficit seemingly impossible to erase with just 11 minutes to play. "It was a tough game," Altidore recalled. "I think Spain underestimated us."

With four minutes left to play, Michael Bradley was ejected following a late tackle on Xavi Alonso. It was the only incident the entire game where the Americans lost their cool. Despite being reduced to 10 men, the United States won the game—leaving the Spanish players in disbelief at the final whistle. While the United States would go on to lose the final, 3–2, against Brazil—after they had been up, 2–0, at the half—the team had made its point. The United States beat Spain and came within 45 minutes of its first FIFA trophy. In an interview with the *New York Times*, Bob Bradley said,

"It's a constant evolution to try to move the team higher and higher so that you have a chance to go to the final and play the best teams and feel confident that you not only belong on the field, but that you can win."

For the first time in national-team history, the Americans were not only a serious contender on the international scene, but also a team that showed it could get results against high-caliber opponents. "I think for us it was a big win, and it will be remembered that way for years," said Altidore. "I really think it helped our confidence going into the World Cup and beyond."

2009 CONCACAF GOLD CUP

With the tournament starting just six days after the Confederations Cup final, Bradley fielded a B-team. The Americans, placed in Group B, with Grenada, Honduras, and Haiti, would come out on top after going 2–1–0. The only blemish was a 2–2 draw against Haiti, a game salvaged by a Stuart Holden goal in stoppage time.

The knockout round posed little challenge, as the United States overcame Panama, 2–1, in the quarterfinals and Honduras, 2–0, in the semifinals. That set up the final against Mexico at Giants Stadium in suburban New York. What the Americans were hoping to be a tight affair turned into a rout. The Americans had done well at Giants Stadium in the past, defeating Panama on penalties to capture the Gold Cup in 2005, and playing Argentina, ranked number one in the world by FIFA at the time, to a 0–0 draw in a 2008 friendly.

What transpired was far from the type of game the Americans will ever want to remember. In what turned into a tale of two halves (the teams were tied 0–0 at halftime), Mexico opened the floodgates on July 26, in front of 79,000 mostly Mexican fans. In the span of just 34 minutes, Mexico scored five times. Inspired by stars Giovani Dos Santos and Carlos Vela, the Mexicans ran roughshod against the U.S. defense. Goalkeeper Troy Perkins did all he could in ensuring Mexico didn't put more balls past him by making five saves, but the effort was not enough. "We ran out of gas, to tell you the truth," Brian Ching told reporters after the game. "It's frustrating. There's nothing else to say. It's a little embarrassing."

Mexico not only won the match, 5–0, to capture the Gold Cup for a fifth time, but it also marked the first time in more than a decade that El Tri had beaten the United States on American soil. The last time had been in San Diego in a 1999 friendly. During that time, Mexico had gone 0–9–2 against the Americans in the United States. The Americans would get another shot at Mexico a few weeks later in a key World Cup qualifier.

Bradley, both apologetic and visibly upset after the game, tried to quell concerns that the Americans were suddenly a team unable to compete. The Americans had come apart—albeit with a different group of players—just a month earlier versus Brazil in the Confederations Cup final. With World Cup qualifying resuming, the Americans could not afford such second-half meltdowns, something Bradley addressed after the defeat to Mexico. "The second half for us is not what we're all about," he told reporters. "When you have a game that feels like this, in the end you don't forget it. It's something that we will always on the inside talk about, be honest about, and hopefully we can use it in a way that we're better from it today. Our focus now is on playing Mexico in Azteca during World Cup qualifying. We start over on that day and have a chance to do something the United States hasn't done before [by winning on Mexican soil]."

2010 WORLD CUP QUALIFYING

The United States, following its great showing at the Confederations Cup, tried to pull off a win on August 12, 2009, versus Mexico at Azteca. Despite taking a 1–0 lead with Davies after just nine minutes, the intense midday heat and the 110,000 fans in attendance did nothing to help the Americans. Instead, it was Mexico who took advantage of the situation with goals from Israel Castro in the 19th minute and Miguel Sabbah in the 82nd to lift Mexico to a 2–1 win. "It's a tough loss to have so many guys work so hard and then give up a late goal," Bradley said during the postgame news conference. "The feeling inside the locker room is one of great disappointment because the idea that you could still walk away with a point after everyone gave everything they had is important for any team."

Despite the loss, the Americans would go on to qualify for the World Cup, downing Honduras, 3–2, in San Pedro Sula on October 10, 2009, in front of a sellout crowd of 37,000. Striker Conor Casey scored two goals—the first two of his national team career—and the United States would finish atop the Hexagonal, edging out Mexico for first place in the region. The Americans' 2–0 victory versus Mexico to open the Hex had given the United States the right momentum during qualifying.

Nonetheless, the team's celebration would be muted heading into its final—and meaningless—game against Costa Rica in Washington, D.C. That game took place October 14, just days after Davies broke a team curfew and had been badly injured in a car accident in northern Virginia. The crash killed a fellow passenger and had put Davies near death. He eventually recovered but would never play for the United States in a World Cup.

LANDON DONOVAN

Widely considered the best player in U.S. soccer history, Landon Donovan had a 14-year national team career that ended in 2014. He was born on March 4, 1982, in Ontario, California. Known for his pace and stamina, Donovan primarily made a name for himself in MLS as a member of the San Jose Earthquakes and later the Los Angeles Galaxy. He also had stints, to varying degrees of success, in both Germany and England. Donovan won a record six MLS Cups and is both the league's all-time scorer, with 145 goals, and leader in assists, with 136. The league's MVP award has been named in his honor.

Career: A member of the inaugural class of the U.S. Soccer Residency Program, Donovan was named tournament MVP at the 1999 FIFA Under-17 World Championship. Soon thereafter, he signed with Bayer Leverkusen of Germany, where he failed to crack the senior team. In 2005, after six years with the German club (most of which he spent on loan to the Earthquakes), Donovan signed with the Galaxy. He retired in 2014, only to return to the Galaxy in 2016. He also spent time playing in Europe, with Bayern Munich (2009) in Germany and Everton (2010 and 2012) in England. He briefly came out of retirement in 2016, playing six games for the Galaxy.

National Team: Donovan is the all-time goals and assists leader for the United States and second-most capped player in history. He is the only player to have scored at least 50 goals and recorded 50 assists, as well as a four-time U.S. Soccer Athlete of the Year winner and a seven-time Honda Player of the Year. He played in the 2002, 2006, and 2010 World Cups. At the 2002 tournament, Donovan was named Best Young Player. In 2010, his three goals at that tournament—including the game-winner versus Algeria—made him the American with the most goals in World Cup history. He is also only one of three Americans—along with Brian McBride and Clint Dempsey—to score in more than one World Cup. He was cut from the U.S. roster ahead of the 2014 World Cup, a decision that ultimately led to his retirement.

Family: Donovan married actress Bianca Kajlich in 2006, but the couple separated in 2009. They divorced a year later. In May 2015, he married Hannah Bartell. The couple welcomed their first child, son Talon, in January 2016.

In the ninth minute of the game against Costa Rica, fans honored Davies by raising placards with the number nine on them, chanting his name, and setting off smoke bombs while the striker recovered in the hospital. The game itself was a seesaw of emotions. The United States fell behind, 2–0, on a rainy night at RFK Stadium, and Onyewu had to come

Photo 8.3. Landon Donovan holds various national team records, including goals scored and assists. (The Steve Nash Foundation)

out of the game on a stretcher in the 83rd minute with a knee injury, which would keep him sidelined for months. But the Americans, forced to play a man short, never surrendered and tied the game with defender Jonathan Bornstein in the fourth minute of stoppage time off a Robbie Rogers corner kick to help the United States win the Hex.

At the same time, the improbable header made Bornstein a hero in Honduras. Bornstein's goal ensured Honduras would finish third, a spot ahead of Costa Rica, to also qualify for the World Cup. In a January 2010 interview with the *New York Times*, Bornstein said he was happy his goal had brought joy to another country. "Growing up, you score goals in club soccer or in college and they maybe help your team win. This goal against Costa Rica had a real impact on a whole nation," he said. "It doesn't just affect me or the team, it affected three countries. That a simple soccer goal could do that is very surreal."

2010 WORLD CUP

Led by Donovan, the United States was as prepared as it would ever be for a World Cup. The United States was placed in Group C, alongside England, Slovenia, and Algeria. It was a tough group but one the Americans were confident they could get out of. A record number of Americans were play- ing in some of Europe's top domestic leagues, and even Donovan, a regular with the Galaxy, had completed a successful loan spell with English club Everton during the winter while MLS lay dormant. Donovan had gained the respect of the English in the months leading up to what would be an epic U.S.–England clash. The match would reveal two things: England's weaknesses (highlighted by the usual pretournament hype that surrounded the home of the Premier League) and the new heights of popularity soccer had achieved in what had forever been a nonsoccer nation. The summer of 2010 would forever change that thanks to the U.S. team and its exploits half a world away.

The United States entered the World Cup with the stated goal of advancing to the knockout stage. Anything less would be a disappointment. In its opening game against England, the U.S. national team had an opponent it knew well. Several Americans—goalkeeper Tim Howard, defender Jay DeMerit, and midfielder Clint Dempsey—played in England. Donovan, the creative force behind the American attack, completed a 10-week winter loan spell with Everton and became an instant fan favorite. "I think the biggest plus for me was gaining the confidence to play at that level consistently. It's one thing to play one good game against a good team, but it's much harder to do it week in and week out," said Donovan. "I feel I am now as prepared as I'll ever be to play in a World Cup."

At the same time, David Beckham had signed with the Galaxy in 2007. He provided MLS with instant star power and gave the league international attention for the first time. Reminiscent of when Pelé signed with the Cosmos, Beckham's arrival was generally seen as a good thing for MLS and growing the game as a whole. Bradley's team had prepared well for their opponents, studying hours of game footage once arriving in South Africa; however, the much-anticipated all-Galaxy clash between Donovan and Beckham would never take place, since the English star had been sidelined earlier in the year, relegated to the bench as part of his country's unofficial role as an assistant coach.

Meanwhile, England was coached by Fabio Capello, an Italian whose refined palate (he is a noted wine connoisseur) and love of art (he has one of the most extensive private collections of paintings in Italy) sets him apart from the beer-drinking English fans who packed into pubs to root for their beloved nation. Also distinguishing Capello was his salary. He earned $9.9 million annually, the highest-paid coach at the tournament. By comparison, Bradley, who loved attending Bruce Springsteen concerts, made $600,000 a year.

The U.S.–England game also revived memories of the 1950 World Cup match, in which the Americans pulled off a shocking 1–0 victory. The team captain at the time, Walter Bahr, became a star in the lead-up to the World Cup. U.S. Soccer was more than happy to trot him out for the fans to see, possibly as a good omen for the Americans who were looking for history to repeat itself. The Americans, with the backing of Nike's marketing machine, released a new jersey ahead of the World Cup, modeled after the 1950 team shirt, replete with a diagonal blue stripe across the front. "The design was nice back in 1950, and I'm glad they went with a similar jersey and used the same one at this World Cup," said Bahr.

The English looked strong in every part of the field except at the goalkeeper position, where Capello was still pondering who to go with just weeks before the U.S. game. None of the three goalies called up by Capello—David James, Joe Hart, or Robert Green—inspired any real confidence in the English backline. This would end up being the team's downfall. For now, the English relished the role of favorite to beat the Americans (and win the group). The United States, in the interim, also had delicate matches against Algeria and Slovenia—teams it had never played before—in its quest to advance. Bradley set up camp at Princeton University in New Jersey, close to the media glare of New York, and even briefly visited President Barack Obama at the White House before jetting off to Johannesburg. Optimism exuded from the U.S. camp. The players were healthy, and the only real and ultimately trivial hiccup was when the team bus was delayed twice by elephants blocking a main road to snack on a few trees. It was a light moment ahead of what would be a tense match.

The Americans took to the field against England on June 12 in Rustenberg, in what was easily the most anticipated match in national team history. What ensued was an inspired U.S. performance and a tough draw that temporarily put both teams atop Group C. After a nervous start, England scored on its first chance when Frank Lampard played the ball into the top of the penalty area that missed Wayne Rooney but found its way to Emile Heskey, who fed the ball to Steven Gerrard. Making a diagonal run into the area ahead of Ricardo Clark, Gerrard one-touched the ball and put it past Howard after just four minutes.

Up 1–0, the English were put back on the defensive as the Americans regained possession and confidence. "I thought we responded well. I thought we were playing well, they were sitting back, and we were creating chances," Dempsey told reporters after the game. Bradley's men evened the score in the 40th minute, when Dempsey grabbed the ball 35 yards from the English goal, faked out Gerrard, and unleashed a powerful left-footed shot that Green failed to hold on to. Instead of making the easy save, the ball trickled over the line for a goal. Dempsey joined McBride as the only players in U.S. soccer history to score in two different World Cup tournaments. "It's one of those goals you always say, 'Why can't I get one like that?' and I'm happy to have scored in both World Cups I've participated in," said Dempsey. The game ended, 1–1, marking the first time since the 1994 World Cup that the United States had opened the tournament with a draw.

In their second game, the Americans faced Slovenia and the defense-first philosophy instilled in its players by coach Matjaz Kek. The strategy had served them well in the past since the team lacked any real stars. But Bradley knew that the heroics that had taken place against England meant nothing if the United States could not get a result against Slovenia. Bradley told reporters at a press conference,

> We've had a good focus the whole time. We've said it so many times that we understand what the first round is about, but we were still excited to start the World Cup playing against England. It's a big game and a big night, and overall we take away positive things as we now get ready for Slovenia.

The game against Slovenia turned out to be another epic encounter for the United States. In another hard-fought game tinged with controversy, the Americans fell behind, 2–0, at halftime on June 18, at Ellis Park. American fans flocked to the game in record numbers, and the crowd support among the 45,573 fans inside the stadium was noticeable. Not to be outdone, the Americans mounted a comeback thanks to second-half goals from Donovan and Michael Bradley. Donovan said the players huddled in the dressing room at halftime, optimistic about tying the score. "We all spoke about first of all believing that we could do it. . . . That was the first thing that was said, and the second was that we need to score as early as we can. We knew if we did that we'd have a chance to get back in the game," he told reporters after the game.

The second half was a new game. The Americans pressured Slovenia's defense early on, with Donovan again spearheading the effort from midfield. It was Donovan who tallied in the 48th minute, after blasting the ball into the roof of the net from close range—a shot that caused Slovenian goalkeeper Samir Handanovic to flinch. The goal, from a mere six yards out, was the culmination of a play that saw Donovan dribble the ball freely along the right flank and into the penalty box, before shooting it into the net from a tight angle for one of the improbable goals. Following a series of failed scoring chances, the Americans tied the score in the 82nd minute on a toe-poke from Bradley, who was set up on the right side by Altidore. After putting the ball into Bradley's path, the midfielder banged in the goal, causing the crowd to erupt in cheers. The U.S. comeback was complete, although what likely would have been the game-winner, scored in the 85th minute by Maurice Edu, was disallowed by Malian referee Koman Coulibaly for no reason. The blown call caused confusion as celebration turned to head-scratching on the field and in the stands. When Coulibaly blew the final whistle, he was surrounded by American players looking for an answer. The referee remained tight-lipped as the players surrounded him. "Who knows what it was? I'm not sure how much English he spoke or if he spoke

English. We asked him several times in a nonconfrontational way. He just ignored us," Donovan said after the game.

Ahead of what would be a decisive match versus Algeria, Americans, for the first time, cared about the fortunes of the team. A win in its final group match on June 23 would automatically earn the Americans a spot in the knockout round. Bradley, however, was focused on his players' fighting spirit and lauded them for their efforts in the first two games. He told reporters during a news conference,

> I think this team has shown that it keeps fighting until the end, and we have now had the experience of pushing games when we're behind. It's a credit to the mentality of the players and to the fact that they're going to fight for 90 minutes every game. We have a third match where we still have the chance to determine our ability to move into the final round.

With Algeria's shocking 0–0 draw against England, the Americans entered the final game in second place, tied with the English on two points but ahead on goals scored (three for the United States and one for England). The United States could also draw against Algeria if England lost to Slovenia. The Americans played Algeria in Pretoria, with the majority of the 35,827 fans in attendance Americans. The most notable attendee was President Bill Clinton, who was using the trip as a chance to hobnob with FIFA president Sepp Blatter in an effort to get the 2022 World Cup to take place in the United States.

Tied 0–0 at halftime, the United States was on the brink of elimination. At the same time, the English were leading Slovenia, 1–0, in Port Elizabeth. The Americans missed several scoring chances, and the frustration was starting to mount. As the clock struck the 90th minute, the United States was in third place and looked to be going home early. As the game entered stoppage time, Howard cleared the ball to Altidore as the Americans launched one final attack. Altidore crossed the ball into the box, and an onrushing Donovan side-footed it into the net for the most dramatic of goals. Donovan celebrated by running toward the corner-kick flag as his teammates, both on the field and from the bench, piled on top of him in jubilation. It was, after Caligiuri's heroics in 1989, the biggest goal in national team history. Caliguri's goal had forever changed the game in the United States; Donovan's goal 21 years later showed the world the U.S. national team was finally part of the game.

By virtue of the win, the Americans had won the group. Donovan became a hero overnight, the goal became a YouTube sensation (it has been viewed more than five million times), and the United States had a new soccer icon. The never-say-die Americans had done it once again. "My favorite memory from that goal was turning the corner and looking up and seeing first Stuart Holden's face running toward the corner flag, followed by like 30 people—including staff and coaches and everyone—and just kind of meeting at the corner flag to celebrate," Donovan recalled. "That was a really cool moment."

Holden corroborated Donovan's recollection, saying, "I was the first one off the bench for every goal celebration (in 2010). Once you realize you won't be playing in a game, you have to make sure you're there for your teammates."

Donovan's last-gasp tally will forever be part of the rich tapestry of highlights and special plays the World Cup has given us throughout the decades. If it hadn't been for the 1994 World Cup played in the United States, Donovan may have never chosen to play soccer. Only 12 at the time, he was at the Rose Bowl when Romania defeated Argentina in the baking California sun. After the Algeria game, Bradley told reporters,

> Without a doubt, Landon has grown in so many different ways. From the soccer end, he mentions the low after the World Cup in 2006. But there was also the challenge of taking a bigger role, being more responsible as a leader. I think these kinds of challenges came at a good time for him, and he's never shied away from challenges.

Photo 8.4.   Landon Donovan celebrates his epic stoppage time goal against Algeria at the 2010 World Cup. (Ben Queenborough/ISI Photos)

Donovan's next challenge was playing Ghana on June 26, in front of 34,976 fans in the round of 16. Although the South Africans in the crowd were pulling for their Ghanaian brothers, U.S. fans made up a good chunk of the group gathered at Royal Bafokeng Stadium that evening. With millions watching in the United States, the Americans, for the first time, perhaps, felt the pressure of the tournament weighing on them. With more exposure came larger responsibility, and Bradley's men were hoping to avoid giving up an early goal as they had in the first two group matches.

Howard was again in the net, with Altidore and striker Robbie Findley up top looking for their first goals of the tournament. Donovan and Dempsey were the force in midfield, aided by Ricardo Clark. Onyewu was relegated to the bench in favor of Jonathan Bornstein, while Michael Bradley was hoping to produce similar heroics as in the Slovenia match. For the Americans, the outcome was not what they had hoped. Ghana powered ahead and gave the Americans a tough game. It was a rematch of a group-stage game won by Ghana in 2006, and the Americans were out for revenge. The loss in Germany four years earlier had eliminated the United States, and the Americans did not want to repeat history.

Photo 8.5. Members of the 2010 World Cup team attend the ESPY Awards in Los Angeles. (Jean Nelson/DepositPhotos)

In the end, Ghana won, 2–1, following an overtime goal by Asamoah Gyan in the 93rd minute. The United States went down after just five minutes. The Americans, as usual, fought back, and Donovan equalized from the penalty spot in the 62nd minute. The loss was stinging. Reaching the quarterfinals had been within their grasp. Donovan lamented to reporters after the game: "There is no guarantee that we'll ever have another opportunity like this ever again in our lifetimes."

9

A New Era:
2011–2016

In recent years, the national team had developed a more rabid follow-ing, particularly in World Cup years, and continued to attract new fans to the sport. MLS celebrated its 20th season in 2015, a time marked by an ever-growing trend of Americans returning to play in the United States after years of plying their trade in Europe. At the same time, a number of German-born players with at least one American parent opted to play for the United States. In the next few years, players like Jermaine Jones, Fabian Johnson, Timothy Chandler, and John Brooks would emerge as starters.

"We've got five players who were born outside the United States be-cause they had a serviceman father who was serving the country," U.S. Soccer president Sunil Gulati told reporters during the 2014 World Cup. "It would be pretty hard to convince me, or anyone else, that they've got less of a right to play for the United States than anyone else."

2011 CONCACAF GOLD CUP

After the 2010 World Cup, the Gold Cup was the first major tournament of the decade for the United States. Again considered a favorite to reach the final alongside Mexico, the Americans, still coached by Bob Bradley, were placed in Group C, with Panama, Canada, and the tiny French terri-tory of Guadeloupe. On June 7, at Detroit's Ford Field, the United States defeated Canada, 2–0, with goals from Jozy Altidore and Clint Dempsey. Four days later, at Raymond James Stadium in Tampa, Florida, the

Americans suffered a rare defeat to Panama, 2–1. It marked the first time in Gold Cup history that the United States had lost a match in group play. The 26-game unbeaten streak had dated back to 1991. "We were a little flat, and they came ready to play," Landon Donovan told reporters after the game. "It's a good learning lesson. We just can't start games like that. Teams are getting better and better in CONCACAF."

In its final first-round game, the United States edged out Guadeloupe, 1–0, on June 14, at Livestrong Park in Kansas City. Altidore tallied the game's only goal after just nine minutes to help the Americans advance to the knockout stage. A relieved Bradley put the team's 2–0–1 record into perspective. "Our goal has always been to get to the final," he told reporters. "We understand from experience what it means in group play. You have to deal with each game and find a way to advance."

The United States, in need of a strong performance, defeated Jamaica, 2–0, on June 19, at RFK Stadium in Washington, D.C. After a scoreless first half, Jones and Dempsey both scored to lift the Americans to victory. The semifinals three days later, at Reliant Stadium in Houston, featured a rematch of the Panama game. Playing in front of 70,000 fans, the United States won, 1–0. Again it was Dempsey who made the difference, in the 76th minute, to get the United States in the final against Mexico.

The final was played during a sunny afternoon on June 25, at the Rose Bowl in Pasadena, California. The 93,000 fans packed into the storied venue witnessed a thrilling meeting between the two rivals. The Americans jumped out to a 1–0 lead when Michael Bradley put them up after just eight minutes. Donovan doubled the lead in the 20th minute off a Dempsey assist. Mexico was down but not out. The Mexicans reacted quickly, as the players—supported by the largely pro-Mexican crowd—pulled one back in the 29th minute with a goal from Pablo Barrera. In the 36th minute, the score was level when Giovanni dos Santos hit a low rocket of a shot to the far post. The ball deflected off Eric Lichaj and bounced to Andrés Guardado's feet. From just eight yards out, Guardado was able to put the ball past Tim Howard to tie the score, 2–2.

After the break, Mexico, with its creativity and exuberant play, continued to hammer the U.S. defense. In the 50th minute, Guardado won the ball near the top of the penalty area, putting in a pass for the darting Barrera. That's when Barrera, who had an excellent game, took a one-time shot that blew past Howard. The United States attempted to respond with three chances of its own—the best being a Carlos Bocanegra header off a Donovan cross and a Dempsey shot that hit the crossbar—but the Mexicans were able to hang on. Mexico put the game away in the 76th minute, when Giovani dos Santos put in a chip shot past Howard to make it 4–2.

"I think sometimes a final becomes a real test of both teams going after each other," said Bob Bradley, adding,

> That was the way we chose to play this game, knowing that it would still require good reactions defensively to deal with those situations . . . there are some plays where our reactions don't end up being as good and sometimes there are some plays where at the end you give credit. Dos Santos's fourth goal was a great piece of skill.

The loss was followed by Bradley's firing, marking the end of a four-year era that featured epic wins versus Spain in the Confederations Cup semifinals and Algeria at the World Cup that helped the team win its first-round group.

Bradley was replaced with Jurgen Klinsmann. Gulati had been eyeing the former German star to coach the United States for a number of years—and finally got him to take the job in July 2011. Klinsmann, the first foreign-born U.S. coach since Milutinovic, promised to reshape the process by which American talent was nurtured and vowed to get better results at such major tournaments as the World Cup. Klinsmann had won the World Cup in 1990, as a player, and coached his country to a third-place finish in 2006. As a player, Klinsmann had a distinguished career with VfB Stuttgart, Inter Milan, and Tottenham Hotspur. As a coach, he had a poor run with Bayern Munich during the 2008–2009 season.

Players at the famed German club had publically criticized Klinsmann for his work habits and training regimen. As coach of the German squad, the German media—upset with him living in California—called on Klinsmann to move to Germany. Klinsmann also drew the ire of critics for his practice of constantly rotating goalkeepers regardless of performance, his poor regard for fielding a strong defense, and his tendency to call in a sports psychologist and nutritionist to work with the players. It was an unorthodox situation, but finishing third at the World Cup silenced his critics.

Some of the criticism Klinsmann endured in Germany followed him to the U.S. job. In March 2013, *Sporting News* published a scathing article criticizing his methods and decisions regarding players. The article read as follows:

> Over the past several weeks, *Sporting News* has spoken to 22 individuals with ties to the U.S. national team or its members—including 11 current players based in MLS or abroad. The remaining sources make their living in American soccer and have reliable relationships with players, coaches, and executives. Sources were offered anonymity in exchange for their anecdotes, observations, and opinions. Those identified by name are Klinsmann and

Photo 9.1.   Jurgen Klinsmann (center) during his playing days with Germany taking on U.S. defender Mike Lapper at the 1993 U.S. Cup. (Jon van Woerden)

three players who spoke shortly before *Sporting News* commenced reporting this story. What emerged over the course of these discussions was near-unanimity regarding the players' flagging faith in Klinsmann, his staff, and his methods, along with the squad's absence of harmony.

With the hiring of Klinsmann, the team saw an influx of German Americans and other players based in Europe. In reality, Klinsmann's recruiting of German Americans was nothing U.S. Soccer and previous coaches had not been doing since the 1990s. Even as the federation used the slogan "One Nation. One Team" to promote the U.S. men's national team, Klinsmann did turn off some in American soccer circles by disparaging MLS and encouraging Americans to sign and play with European clubs. The real problem for the American game, however, wasn't players going to Europe, but the country's failure to produce more talent. Hispanic Americans, largely ignored by U.S. Soccer, continued to be an untapped resource. In addition, the program's inability to achieve any success at the U-17, U-20, and Olympic team levels with Klinsmann at the helm highlighted his limitations as the national team's technical director and senior team coach.

Of the players born outside the United States, Jones was the one who Klinsmann would build his midfield around. Born in Germany to an American father and German mother, Jones had played for Germany at the Under-21 and senior team levels but never in an official FIFA-sanctioned tournament. He had been part of the fold under Bradley and made his debut in August 2010, against Poland. A veteran of the German league with such teams as Bayer Leverkusen and Schalke 04, Jones joined MLS in 2014, after signing with the New England Revolution. The move was in direct contrast to Klinsmann's order that Americans needed to play in Europe to develop. Instead, a trend emerged of more Americans returning to MLS, while many—like college star Jordan Morris—also opted to play domestically.

2013 CONCACAF GOLD CUP

Just a year out from the World Cup, Klinsmann used the Gold Cup to prepare the team for his first major tournament at the helm of the U.S. squad. Placed in Group C, alongside Costa Rica, Cuba, and Belize, the United States was looking to string together a good showing. The Americans did not disappoint, trouncing Belize, 6–1, on July 9, in Portland, and cruising past Cuba, 4–1, just four days later in Sandy, Utah. Costa Rica, the most difficult of the opening-round opponents for the United States, proved manageable in the end. The Americans defeated them, 1–0, on July 16, thanks to a goal from Brek Shea with eight minutes left to play at Rentschler Field in East Hartford, Connecticut. The victory helped set an all-time record for consecutive wins—eight in all—as the Americans rolled on to the knockout stage.

The wins kept on coming on July 21, after the United States defeated El Salvador, 5–1, at M&T Bank Stadium in Baltimore. Donovan recorded a goal and three assists in front of 70,540 fans pleased with Klinsmann's work. For Donovan, the Gold Cup was proving a success after taking a three-month hiatus earlier in the year. Although the break came much to the chagrin of Klinsmann, it proved energizing to the overworked Donovan. For the team, it was yet another rout—a confidence-boosting win for Klinsmann as he tried to put his imprint on a team still looking for an identity. Klinsmann vowed to instill a winning mentality and a unique playing style in a national team never known to have one. If this Gold Cup was any indication, the coach wanted his team to be offensively astute, while never underestimating an opponent. "I think it's important that we sent out the signals right at the beginning of this game," Klinsmann told reporters. "To be honest, the only team that can really lose is us. We all expect, the fans expect, for us to win the game. These teams are not easy to play. That's why you need to take it very seriously."

Although the Gold Cup was no measure of the sort of competition the United States would meet at the World Cup, Klinsmann pressed the point that his team was "trying to catch up with the big teams in the world" that had been enjoying success for decades. "If you raise the bar, it's all about speed," he told reporters. "I'm not talking about physical speed. I'm talking about mental speed, passing speed. It's about compactness, about going both ways the same way with 11 players involved, offensively, defensively. That's what we're working on." The Americans had defeated some stiff competition during several friendlies in 2012—a 1–0 victory against Italy in Genoa and 1–0 versus Mexico at Estadío Azteca. That historic victory was the first time the United States had defeated its rival on Mexican soil. Earlier in 2013, the Americans had also defeated Germany, 4–3, in Washington, D.C.

While the United States wasn't going to turn into Brazil overnight, Klinsmann viewed the Gold Cup, with its many matches crammed into a tight schedule, as a great way to prepare for the World Cup. On July 24, the United States dismantled Honduras, 3–1, at Cowboys Stadium in Dallas, to reach its fifth straight Gold Cup final. It was a day of records, as Donovan tallied two goals and recorded an assist to give the United States its 10th consecutive win. In five Gold Cup games, the United States was undefeated, outscoring opponents 19–4.

The self-imposed sabbatical had seemingly reenergized Donovan, whose team-leading five goals and seven assists got the squad to the title game. "I've never been part of a run like this," Donovan told the *Los Angeles Times*. "It's a lot of fun, not only the goals, but we're creating lots of chances, and that's enjoyable." Even Klinsmann had taken note of Donovan's heroics. After Donovan's winter break, Klinsmann told reporters he would have to earn his way back into consideration for a spot on the World Cup roster. "For us coaches, it's important to see a difference-maker out there who, when maybe things go a little bit the wrong way, they take the game on their feet," the coach told reporters when asked about Donovan after the quarterfinals. "Landon was one of those players."

Up next for the United States was a clash versus Panama in the final at Chicago's Soldier Field for a shot at lifting the Gold Cup once again. Panama had shocked Mexico, 2–1, in the semifinals. Although it had never won the Gold Cup, Panama had a decent history of stunning opponents at the tournament, particularly in the knockout rounds. But the United

States, too strong and on a roll, edged Panama, 1–0, on July 28, playing for a crowd of 57,920. Again, it was Shea who made the difference, the lanky midfielder scoring the game's only goal in the 69th minute. The goal, scored just 42 seconds after coming off the bench, gave the United States its fifth Gold Cup and 11th straight victory. Talking with reporters after the game, Donovan expressed his hope that Klinsmann would include him in future games. "This is not the end. This is just the end of the tournament, but hopefully this is just the beginning for a lot of us, and we want to be part of the bigger picture," he said.

Although excited about the win, Klinsmann tried to put it into perspective. "The global game is played in South America and it's played in Europe and there are a lot of other benchmarks waiting for us," he said at the postgame news conference, "but it's time that you see progress from this group of players. They all understand that it takes a lot more to become really good." Klinsmann also made the bold statement that soccer had officially made it as a major sport in the United States:

> Soccer in this country is unstoppable—you can't stop it anymore. It will get only better. It will get bigger. The crowds we've had at the last three games were 60, 70, 80,000 in Dallas, in Baltimore, people buying into this sport. Millions of kids play in this country. Do we need to improve many elements in the game? Yes, we all know that. You can't stop it anymore. Soccer has made it here in the United States.

2014 WORLD CUP QUALIFYING

There had been a time when the United States had struggled to compete with the teams in its region. But that was far from the case now. The United States dominated the region, and qualifying for the World Cup was no longer a question of "if." The United States, under Klinsmann this time, would win the Hexagonal, finishing ahead of Costa Rica, Honduras, and Mexico.

The qualifying tournament was highlighted by two home matches—a clash against Costa Rica and the much-anticipated game against Mexico. Both matches were won by the United States thanks to some gamesmanship—the ability to defeat opponents in cold weather. The calendar may have signaled that March 23, 2013, was the third day of spring, but it was anything but in Denver. The city was enveloped by a massive blizzard, and Dick's Sporting Goods Park in Commerce City, where the game was scheduled to be played, was covered in the white stuff. The Americans were winless at this point in the Hex, and the game was a must-win for Klinsmann, who had come under fire in recent months.

By the time the game was to start, some 20 inches had fallen on Denver. Costa Rican officials argued the contest should not be played, but the match officials refused to postpone the game. In front of a sellout crowd of 19,374, the United States defeated Costa Rica, 1–0. The deluge of snow and an icy field were too much for Costa Rica to handle. Also too much for Costa Rica was Dempsey, who scored the game-winner in the 16th minute. Brad Guzan, playing for the injured Howard, made five saves to preserve the shutout.

In the 55th minute, as the snow continued to fall, it looked as if the game would be halted. Play was briefly stopped as FIFA's match commissioner and referee Joel Aguilar of El Salvador met on the sidelines—surrounded by players from both teams—to discuss the playing conditions. After a few minutes, the referee ordered the grounds crew, who had been busy throughout the game, to clean the snow off the lines. Play would continue.

The United States—wearing its "continental jersey" in honor of U.S. Soccer and the team's 100th anniversary—had finally put together a strong performance. The game would come to be known as the "Snow-clasico." Costa Rica, meanwhile, filed an appeal with CONCACAF, but it was later dismissed. "That was not our fault," Klinsmann told the *New York Times*. "I didn't call God to give us some snow."

The win put the United States in second place in the Hex ahead of its road match versus Mexico just three days later. In what felt like a victory, the Americans escaped with a 0–0 draw at Estadío Azteca. It would be a victory against Mexico, however, on September 10, in Columbus, that would qualify the United States for the World Cup. Again it was a *dos a cero* that decided the match. A loud, pro-U.S. crowd propelled the Americans to victory—not to mention goals from Eddie Johnson in the 49th minute and Donovan just 11 minutes from the end for the 2–0 win. The victory, combined with Honduras tying Panama, 2–2, in Tegucigalpa an hour later, gave the United States its seventh straight World Cup berth and the 10th in its history.

It was also a night for personal records. With the goal and an assist, Donovan broke his national-team points record for a calendar year, with 24, in 2013 (eight goals and eight assists), outdoing his previous points mark of 22 in 2007 (nine goals and four assists). The issues highlighted by *Sporting News* had appeared to be a nonfactor in the lead-up to the World Cup. Despite some problems, the players appeared unified and the talent pool deeper than ever. Klinsmann had juggled the lineup many times looking for the right combination, but in the end he had achieved success. Although trouble awaited him, the aura around the coach was nothing but positive as the team prepared for the World Cup finals.

CLINT DEMPSEY

One of the finest talents the United States has produced in the modern era, Clint Dempsey is also one the most prolific strikers this country has ever seen. Born in Nacogdoches, Texas, Dempsey learned to play soccer as a child, growing up in the predominantly Mexican American community. Nicknamed "Deuce," Dempsey's game combines athleticism and creativity. He also holds several national-team records, including scoring the second-most goals in history with 56. Dempsey's 132 caps are the fourth-most in national-team history. He also played in three World Cups (2006, 2010, and 2014). Dempsey is a three-time U.S. Soccer Male Athlete of the Year.

Career: Dempsey got his start in MLS with the New England Revolution. He was named MLS Rookie of the Year in 2004, after being drafted eighth overall in the SuperDraft after completing his junior year at Furman. In 2006, Dempsey transferred to English club Fulham, tallying 50 goals in 184 games; however, his most famous goal came in 2009–2010, in the Europa League, when he scored a spectacular long chip-shot goal against Juventus of Italy. Dempsey would go on to become the first American to play in a major European final in May 2010, when Fulham lost to Atletico Madrid of Spain. In August 2012, Dempsey transferred to fellow London club Tottenham Hotspur, where he scored seven goals in 29 appearances during the 2012–2013 season. At the end of the campaign, he returned to MLS and signed with Seattle Sounders FC. In his three seasons with Seattle, Dempsey has scored 34 goals in 72 games, while leading the team to the U.S. Open Cup in 2014. For Dempsey, the title was the first major piece of silverware he won as a professional player. He was sidelined for the remainder of the season in 2016, after he was diagnosed with an irregular heartbeat—the same year the Sounders won MLS Cup.

National Team: Dempsey made his U.S. debut in 2004, versus Jamaica, and quickly emerged as one of the team's best players. He has played in three World Cups (2006, 2010, and 2014). At the 2010 World Cup, Dempsey became only the second American (after Brian McBride) to score in more than one game when he tallied against England. In March 2013, he was named team captain. At the 2014 World Cup, Dempsey scored against Ghana after just 29 seconds, the fastest goal by an American in World Cup history and fifth fastest all-time in World Cup history. With this goal, Dempsey also became the first American player to score in three consecutive World Cups.

Family: Dempsey is married to Bethany Keegan Dempsey. They have four children, two sons and two daughters. In his free time, he is an avid fisherman and likes to produce rap music.

Photo 9.2   Clint Dempsey (Major League Soccer)

2014 WORLD CUP

The United States was drawn into one of the World Cup's toughest groups and would travel to Brazil to face three teams with intriguing connections to the national team. Ghana had eliminated the United States from the last two World Cups; Portugal had been the team the Americans had defeated in a stunning upset at the 2002 tournament; and Germany was the team Klinsmann had coached at the 2006 World Cup. "We will be meeting old friends. It is already something special to have the USA in our group. Jurgen and I have had a very good and close relationship for a long time," Germany coach Joachim Löw, who had served as Klinsmann's assistant, told reporters following the draw.

Aside from the challenge Group G offered, the United States was also the team that had to travel the most between its three first-round matches. Making the situation potentially worse was that the Americans were scheduled to play Portugal in the city of Manaus in a newly built venue located deep in the jungles of the Amazon. The weather conditions—tropical and wet—awaited both teams. "We don't complain. We take it on. We do the traveling, and we adjust to the climate. This is what a World Cup is about. It's about these challenges. It's exciting in certain ways and a big challenge. That's what we want," the ever-optimistic Klinsmann told reporters.

On the eve of the tournament, Klinsmann shocked fans and journalists alike when he decided to leave Donovan off the World Cup roster. The sabbatical Donovan had taken (during which time he had spent a year in Cambodia) had clearly bothered Klinsmann. The exclusion ignited a social media firestorm and criticism—on both sides of the argument—about whether Klinsmann had made the correct decision. Upon his exclusion, Donovan released a statement, saying, "I firmly believe that not only should I be going, but I feel like I really deserved it."

The Americans needed to defeat Ghana in their opener in Natal if they had any hope of advancing. They were ultimately successful. Dempsey wasted no time putting the United States ahead, scoring just 30 seconds after the opening whistle—the fifth-fastest goal in World Cup history—following a dazzling run in the box. Needing just four touches, Dempsey got past two Ghana defenders before blasting the ball into the net.

The Americans were hoping the goal would be enough to win the match, especially after Jozy Altidore pulled a hamstring and had to be substituted midway through the first half. Instead, the U.S. defense gave up a goal in the 82nd minute, when Andre Ayew knocked the ball inside the left post and past Howard. The United States had spent much of the second half fending off attacks and struggled to create any offense. That all changed on a set piece. With four minutes left in the game, defender John Brooks, on as a halftime substitute after Matt Besler left the game with hamstring tightness, headed home the winner off a Graham Zusi corner kick. A surprised Brooks celebrated the goal—his hands on his head with a look of shock on his face—by laying facedown on the grass as his teammates piled on top of him. Brooks said afterward that he had dreamed of scoring the game-winner the previous day. "I thanked God for the great moment," he told reporters after the match.

The goal unleashed wild celebrations in the stands—where a large American fan contingent had convened, including Vice President Joe Biden—and gave the team a much-needed three points to start the tournament. Klinsmann said in the postgame press conference that he "was still convinced we were going to win this game even after [Ghana] got the equalizer." He added, "I had the feeling that another two or three chances would come, and we would need just one of those opportunities, which then happened. This is definitely the result we wanted. The players worked hard for it."

The second match played by the United States, versus Portugal on June 24, in Manaus, would also prove to be a tough test. Klinsmann's men took on a Portugal side that featured an injured Cristiano Ronaldo, but Portugal nonetheless took the lead with a Nani goal after just five minutes, following a poorly played ball by Geoff Cameron. Both teams appeared sluggish for stretches of the first half, and the humidity of the jungle made it unbearable at times. In the 39th minute, referee Nestor Pitana of Argentina whistled for a water break, the first in World Cup history. The United States had struggled in the first half but dominated the start of the second. Jermaine Jones tied the score in the 65th minute, when his 27-yard shot off the right post found the back of the net. "We discussed at halftime with all the players. We said, 'It's all good guys, we're going to get this first goal, then we're going to get a second goal,'" Klinsmann told reporters.

With the game tied, 1–1, the Americans grew confident. Ronaldo, who had been named FIFA's Player of the Year in January, was invisible for much of the game, and the U.S. midfield, spearheaded by Zusi and Kyle Beckerman, helped move the ball forward. Michael Bradley, who had been expected to help generate offense, was out of sorts—something that would come to highlight the type of World Cup he would go on to have. But Klinsmann's mantra was the group over the individual. "It's not going to be a perfect game all the time. I'm not expecting perfect games from anybody. I expect they give everything they have and then when he makes a mistake that the other guy is there to help him out," Klinsmann said of his team during a news conference.

Coming up big once again was Dempsey. He connected with a Zusi cross in the 81st minute and scored his second goal of the tournament. Up 2–1, the Americans knew that a victory would automatically put them through to the second round. But Portugal's Silvestre Varela, off a perfectly placed Ronaldo cross, scored past Howard for the tying goal in the fifth minute of stoppage time to ruin the party. The game ended, 2–2. "If we would have said starting the tournament with four points after the first two games, we would have been really happy about it. Obviously when you get a goal [against you] in the last seconds of the game when you have pretty much six points then it's a bummer for a moment that you have to swallow," Klinsmann told reporters after the game. "But, it was an outstanding game by all the players."

The final group game played by the United States, against Germany, would be decisive. Win and go through; a draw and even a loss were still possibilities the United States could bank on depending on the outcome of the Portugal–Ghana match. Weather once again was a factor. The June 26 match in Recife was marred by heavy rain from the day before. With the weather appearing to worsen just hours before kickoff, the streets surrounding the stadium and throughout the fifth-largest Brazilian city were knee-deep in water. Thousands braved the flooded streets to get to the game. The 12-hour downpour may have created havoc, but the stadium's drainage system ensured that the game could go on, and an inspection of the pitch by match officials confirmed that no delay would occur.

Rain could not keep away the thousands of American fans—and their "I Believe That We Will Win" chant, which had permeated stadiums in the previous two games played by the United States. Aside from the growing number of Americans in Brazil, the following back home had grown to never-before-seen levels for soccer. Bars, restaurants, and public parks had become places for people to gather. Although many had never even watched a soccer game before, it seemed—temporarily at least—that World Cup fever had caught on. On the field, the Americans lost, 1–0, but the team managed to reach the knockout round after Portugal's 2–1 win against Ghana. The lone goal came in the 55th minute, from German striker Thomas Muller. After the final whistle, Klinsmann and Löw hugged on the sidelines. The outcome meant the United States would play Belgium, the winner of Group H.

The match versus Belgium took place on July 1, in Salvador, in front of a crowd of 51,227 fans, many of them Americans. Excitement for the United States had reached an all-time high. A win would equal the team's showing at the 2002 World Cup, while a loss would be no better than what had been accomplished four years earlier in South Africa. With the hype surrounding Klinsmann also reaching an all-time high, the pressure was on the former German international to get the Americans into the quarterfinals. The United States had hoped to get Altidore back for the match, but he would remain out of the game after days of speculation that he could be used as a sub. Instead, Klinsmann went with Dempsey, flanked up top alongside Alejandro Bedoya and Fabian Johnson.

On the other side of the field, Belgium was not lacking in offensive firepower. In the end, the Americans, full of energy and armed with a late comeback in their arsenal, came up short. Nevertheless, it was Howard who spent the evening trying to block everything put in his path. And he almost did. Klinsmann's men held on for dear life as Belgium created waves of scoring chances. Despite that, it was the Americans who could have won the game in the 90th minute, when Chris Wondolowski, positioned near the Belgian goal, blasted his shot high. The game went to overtime tied, 0–0.

Three minutes into extra time, Belgium's Romelu Lukaku dribbled from midfield to the right side of the box. Defender Omar Gonzalez failed to properly clear the ball, allowing Kevin De Bruyne to fire a shot. Howard was unable to stretch out his right leg far enough to stop the ball, and Belgium was up, 1–0. In the 105th minute, Belgium seemed to put the game out of reach when Lukaku, off a De Bruyne pass, beat Howard from six yards out. The game appeared over—but not for the United States. Klinsmann put in Julian Green, a fresh attacking player, in an effort to score a goal. Green, who sat on the bench for Bayern Munich's youth team, had been a controversial choice to make the roster, especially after Donovan had been excluded. Green had been born in Tampa, Florida, but moved back to Germany, the country of his mother's birth, when he

Photo 9.3. Goalkeeper Tim Howard stretches to make a save against Belgium at the 2014 World Cup. (Perry McIntyre/ISI Photos)

was just two. Sought out by both the United States and Germany, he had opted to play for the U.S. men's national team.

Getting minutes on the world's biggest stage was Green's chance to show everyone how much of an impact the budding striker could make during a big game. That's exactly what Green did in the 107th minute, connecting with a perfectly placed Bradley ball to volley it into the net. The goal put the Americans within one; however, the Belgians controlled the pace and managed to win, 2–1.

Howard was the hero of the night, recording 16 saves—the most ever in a World Cup game—but it hadn't been enough to see the Americans through. "This was definitely an amazing goalkeeper performance. There is no doubt about it. He should be very proud of himself, and we are proud to have him with us," Klinsmann told reporters after the game. The saves, however, were little consolation for Howard. "It's heartbreaking. I don't think we could have given any more," he said. "What a great game. . . . We left it all out there. We got beat by a really good team. They took their chances well. It's heartache. It hurts."

Donovan, not afraid to criticize Klinsmann after his exclusion from the team, told MLSSoccer.com that the loss had "disappointed" him. "I think we're all disappointed in what happened. I think the most disappointing thing is we didn't seem like we gave it a real effort, from a tactical stand-point. I thought the guys did everything they could, they did everything that was asked of them, but I don't think we were set up to succeed, and that was tough to watch."

Despite the defeat, the team had captured the imagination of an entire country. For the first time, it looked as if the entire nation cared about soccer and the fortunes of the U.S. team.

2015 CONCACAF GOLD CUP

The United States entered the Gold Cup in need of winning it. By virtue of having won the event two years earlier, another victory would auto-matically qualify the team for the 2017 Confederations Cup. If the squad was to lose the tournament, it would be forced into a tiebreaker against the 2015 champion. Instead, the United States had an average tourna-ment. Klinsmann was criticized for constantly experimenting with line-ups throughout the first round. The team failed to come together when it needed to, and the result was crashing out of the tournament in the semifinals.

The United States fell to Jamaica on July 22, in Atlanta. Playing in front of 70,511 onlookers at the Georgia Dome, the Americans suffered a shock-ing defeat as Jamaica scored twice in the first half—one goal on a blunder by Guzan—to ultimately win the game. It was the first loss suffered by the United States to a Caribbean nation since a 1969 defeat at the hands of Haiti. It marked the first time the United States was eliminated by a CONCACAF team en route to the Gold Cup final. Darren Mattocks gave Jamaica the lead with a 31st-minute header directly off a throw-in. Giles Barnes followed that up five minutes later with a goal on an 18-yard free kick after Guzan was caught outside the penalty area on what should have been a routine throw.

Klinsmann was on the hot seat. Some called for his ousting, although U.S. Soccer confirmed it had confidence in him. The Americans had even dominated for long stretches of the match and tried in vain throughout the second half to push the game to overtime after Bradley's goal in the 47th minute. "We had enough chances to put three or four or five in there," Klinsmann told reporters after the match. "We didn't do it. That's why we lost." The United States would finish the tournament in fourth place.

2015 CONCACAF CUP

Mexico defeated Jamaica, 3–1, in the Gold Cup final, forcing CONCA-CAF to schedule a tiebreaker match. The game between the United States and Mexico would be played on October 10, 2015, at the Rose Bowl. Tickets for the one-game playoff were allocated evenly to American and Mexican fans, and the winner would qualify for the Confederations Cup. The game itself proved to be another classic in the ongoing rivalry.

In front of a crowd of 93,723, Mexico defeated the United States, 3–2, in a nail-biting game that was resolved in extra time. It was the second-largest crowd to ever watch a U.S. national team game. The United States twice came from behind to equalize at 2–2 in the 108th minute, which appeared to be enough to send the game to penalty kicks. Instead, Paul Aguilar's spectacular one-time volley, which went past Guzan in the 118th, proved to be the game-winner. Aguilar ran to the sidelines and dove onto the crowd as his teammates piled on top of him in celebration.

The outcome was more bad news for Klinsmann and gave more ammunition to those who had been calling for his ouster. Again, U.S. Soccer confirmed it was not planning to replace Klinsmann. It was his first loss to Mexico in seven games as U.S. coach. Nothing seemed to be going his way since the World Cup. Had the man tasked with revolutionizing the American game failed his mandate? He had a year—at the Copa America Centenario—to prove his growing chorus of critics wrong.

2016 COPA AMERICA CENTENARIO

The Copa America turned 100 years old, the oldest continental soccer tournament in the world, and both South American and CONCACAF officials decided to have the United States host a special edition of the competition. It was the biggest competition involving national teams since the United States had hosted the 1994 World Cup and 1999 Women's World Cup. Although the tournament had initially been mired in a wide-ranging corruption scandal involving FIFA officials and various marketing executives, the event—in jeopardy of being called off—came together just in time for the summer of 2016.

The United States, as host nation, was placed in Group A, with Colombia, Costa Rica, and Paraguay. For Klinsmann's team, it was a tough group. It was also an opportunity for the United States to get back to its winning ways after a disappointing 2015. Despite the optimism on the eve of the tournament, the U.S. loss to Colombia in the tournament opener on June 2, at Levi's Stadium in Santa Clara, California, was reason for concern. The Americans looked lost for much of the 2–0 defeat, the South Americans too strong for Klinsmann's group. Both goals were off set pieces, something the Americans had a tough time defending against. The United States went down early—Cristian Zapata scoring in the eighth minute on a play born from a corner kick—with Guzan, the preferred starter to Howard on the bench, giving up the goal. A sloppy DeAndre Yedlin handball in the box later in the first half allowed James Rodriguez to score on the ensuing penalty kick in the 42nd minute. Yedlin, a defender with Seattle Sounders FC, ended up signing a contract with Tottenham in England after the World Cup. The United States, meanwhile, had only one strong scoring chance in the 60th minute: Dempsey's powerful header was cleared off the line by Sebastian Perez near the post.

After just one game, the United States found itself in a must-win situation if it hoped to advance to the next round. Up next was a familiar opponent, Costa Rica, on June 7, at Soldier Field in Chicago. Klinsmann's team used the CONCACAF opponents as a punching bag, regrouping from the Colombia defeat to win, 4–0, with Clint Dempsey (his 50th career goal for the United States), Jermaine Jones, Bobby Wood, and Graham Zusi scoring the goals. It had been the performance Klinsmann had asked for from his players. The U.S. backline of DeAndre Yedlin, Geoff Cameron, John Brooks, and Fabian Johnson put in a strong showing, as Costa Rica was unable to get anything going offensively. After a year of experiments, this seemed to be the four-man defense Klinsmann was going with for the rest of the tournament. In addition, there was a lot of buzz surrounding Christian Pulisic, a 17-year-old playing with German club Borussia Dortmund who Klinsmann was hoping to integrate into the team. Whether Pulisic would be able to live up to those expectations remained to be seen.

The win moved the United States temporarily into first place with a game left to play in the first round. On June 11, the United States faced Paraguay at Lincoln Financial Field in Philadelphia. Paraguay had proved to be a tough side at past Copa America tournaments and was exactly the type of team the United States needed to measure itself against to see how far it had come under Klinsmann. Once again, it was Dempsey who was the hero of the night, his goal after 27 minutes giving the Americans a 1–0 win. The Americans were on an emotional high. Indeed, never have two consecutive victories brought so much promise when it came to the team's future. The Copa America Centenario had suddenly become the place where the United States was making its case as one of the strongest teams in the Americas.

It was more than grabbing six points from two must-win games. It had been the overall context. As Klinsmann had argued, the outcome was not an underdog story, but part of a gradual and natural evolution that had seen the team grow during the past few years. "We showed a lot of heart and character," Dempsey told reporters after the hard-fought win versus Paraguay. "I'm excited to be out of the group. Hopefully we can build on this win and move forward."

The United States had entered the Paraguay game needing just a point to reach the Copa Centenario's knockout stage. They took three points, winning Group A after Costa Rica downed Colombia. It also put the team a step closer to Klinsmann's stated goal at the start of the tournament: the semifinals. For Klinsmann, the tournament was always about winning knockout games. That's what would prepare the team for similar scenarios at the 2018 World Cup in Russia. "It's just a wonderful opportunity for our team to play these types of games," Klinsmann said during a press conference for the knockout round that immediately followed the Paraguay game, not yet knowing who the next opponent would be for the United States. "We want to get certain experiences to get this growth in our mindset that we can compete."

The players had come to understand the importance of playing competitive matches. More importantly, they knew that they had to win these games. After being eliminated from the World Cup two straight times in the round of 16, the Copa presented the opportunity for the players to show themselves, Klinsmann, and the world they could win high-stakes matches. By virtue of the loss to Colombia in the opener, the team's two remaining first-round games had essentially become do-or-die scenarios.

With their backs against the wall, the Americans responded. It was the team's never-say-die attitude—the kind seen under Bob Bradley a few years earlier—that came through once again. Building on positive results had been something Klinsmann and his staff had been attempting to do since

U.S. Soccer hired him in 2011. This was a team yearning to win more, especially after the previous year's loss to Jamaica in the Gold Cup semifinals and its failure to qualify for the Confederations Cup with a loss to Mexico. Playing in the Confederations Cup would have served as a wonderful dress rehearsal for the World Cup. As a result, the tournament had suddenly become the perfect setting for the Americans to shock the world.

The 2–0 loss to Colombia, while not entirely shocking, did sting. The Americans—who played with the same starting lineup in three straight games at this tournament for the first time since the 1930 World Cup—were able to shake off the defeat. They coming out strong versus Costa Rica and scored early to put that game away. Ditto versus Paraguay. While not always pretty (whether it was a 4–3–3 that turned into a 4–1–3–2 or a traditional 4–4–2), the team got the job done. Even down a man against Paraguay for nearly the entire second half after Yedlin was red-carded, the United States remained undeterred. Klinsmann's use of the same starting lineup in all three games injected confidence into this team. It also showed that Klinsmann was convinced this was the group he could rely on—with the occasional insertion of Graham Zusi, Darlington Nagbe, and Christian Pulisic—as the tournament progressed. While everyone remained curious about the potential of Nagbe and Pulisic, it had been the play of veterans like Dempsey that made all the difference. The use of one-touch passing to create offense had also been one component of the team's recent success.

The United States was pitted against Ecuador in the quarterfinals on June 16, in Seattle. Ecuador was another manageable opponent for the Americans, but this time Klinsmann was forced to change his lineup due to suspensions. Yedlin was out of the game due to his red card, replaced by Matt Besler in the back. With a loud crowd of 47,322 at CenturyLink Park supporting the Americans, the United States took the lead after 22 minutes, thanks to a Dempsey header. The Americans took that lead into halftime, but cards started to take a toll on both teams. In the 52nd minute, both sides had players red-carded, as Antonio Valencia received a second caution for Ecuador and Jones earned a straight red for an off-the-ball incident. Nonetheless, both sides remained lively, and it was the United States that scored an assurance goal in the 65th minute from Gyasi Zardes.

Brooks and Cameron made sure to sweep away any of Ecuador's forays at Guzan's goal, although the South Americans did pull one back in the 74th minute with a goal from Michael Arroyo. It was his one-time shot, off a corner kick, that got past Guzan for the only blemish of the game. But the victory had come with a hangover. Jermaine Jones (red card), Bobby Wood, and Alejandro Bedoya (accumulated yellows) were suspended for the semifinals against Argentina. But that didn't put a damper on the victory. Klinsmann had succeeded in getting his team to the semifinals for the first time since the 1995 Copa America. The sense in the dressing room was that this team could accomplish almost anything. "This was a huge step forward," Klinsmann told reporters.

The U.S.'s semifinal opponent was Argentina. Argentina was not only one of the best teams in the world and a pretournament favorite to capture the title, but also home to Lionel Messi, the best player on the planet. Klinsmann's men would have to conjure up something really special if they wanted to reach the final. That would not be the case. The Americans were sent back to Earth on June 21, at NRG Stadium in Houston, when Messi showed everyone the soccer genius he can be. Behind Messi's mastery, Argentina defeated the United States, 4–0. Messi was part of three of his team's goals. He set up the first goal with a quick pass to Ezequiel Lavezzi in the third minute, scored the second goal on a perfectly placed free kick later in the first half, and scooped up a loose ball in front of Guzan's goal in the 86th minute and fed it to Gonzalo Higuaín for Argentina's fourth goal. The game was essentially over after that first goal. "After that early goal," Klinsmann observed at a news conference after the game, "I think our players could feel that, probably at every position on the field, [Argentina] was just better than we are." The United States would finish the tournament in fourth place. The Americans had come so far—especially in the modern era—yet still had new heights to reach.

But a poor start to the final round of World Cup qualifying—losses to Mexico and Costa Rica in November 2016, to open the Hexagonal—cost Klinsmann his job. The German had failed at his mandate. Tasked with overhauling and changing the national team, he had not been the transformative figure Gulati had hoped for when he hired him in 2011. Klinsmann had been the biggest critic of the U.S. soccer program, but in the end he did little to fix it. For the few ups the team had, there had been too many downs. The elimination by Jamaica at the Gold Cup, the 4–0 loss to Argentina in the semifinals, and the 0–2 start ended the Klinsmann era. Whatever progress there was had been too incremental. Klinsmann's tactics and habitually changing lineups had come back to haunt him. The 2–1 loss to Mexico in Columbus, which broke the string of *dos a cero* results, and the 4–0 road loss to Costa Rica were the final straws. U.S. Soccer named Bruce Arena to replace Klinsmann, the second time the Hall of Fame coach would take over the national team.

With the 2018 World Cup still on the horizon, the United States has become an established regional power, with passionate fans and players who have their sights set on someday winning it. A lot of work still needs to be done. The quality gap still needs to be filled. Technique, athleticism, and skill remain facets of the game American players and the national team still need to combine for a cohesive recipe for success. It should be noted that American soccer has come a long way. How far it can still go is something we will learn in the coming years and decades.

Appendix A

All-Time Records

TEAM STREAKS

Most consecutive wins overall: 12
  June 2, 2013–August 14, 2013
Most consecutive wins in the United States: 13
  June 2, 2013–February 1, 2014
Most consecutive wins outside the United States: 3
  November 15, 2011–February 29, 2012
Most consecutive games unbeaten overall: 16
  March 13, 2004–March 19, 2005
Most consecutive games unbeaten in the United States: 16
  January 19, 2008–July 23, 2009
Most consecutive games unbeaten outside the United States: 6
  March 31, 2004–February 9, 2005
Most consecutive losses overall: 12
  October 16, 1973–August 25, 1975
Most consecutive losses in the United States: 5
  June 19, 1949–March 28, 1959
Most consecutive losses outside the United States: 11
  October 16, 1973–August 25, 1975
Most consecutive shutouts earned overall: 6
  June 8, 2008–September 10, 2008
Most consecutive shutouts against overall: 5
  November 18, 1990–February 21 1991

GAMES

Most goals scored: 8
  November 14, 1993; USA 8, Cayman Islands 1
  June 15, 2008; USA 8, Barbados 0
Most goals scored, defeat: 3
  August 17, 1930; Brazil 4, USA 3
  September 19, 1937; Mexico 7, USA 3
  June 8, 1953; England 6, USA 3
  June 13, 1993; Germany 4, USA 3
Most goals allowed: 11
  May 30, 1928; Argentina 11, USA 2
  August 6, 1948; Norway 11, USA 0
Most goals allowed, win: 3
  October 20, 1968; USA 6, Haiti 3
  October 8, 1995; USA 4, Saudi Arabia 3
  August 14, 2013; USA 4, Bosnia-Herzegovina 3
  June 5, 2015; USA 4, Netherlands 3
Most goals, both teams: 13
  May 20, 1928; Argentina 11, USA 2
Largest margin of victory: 8
  June 15, 2008; USA 8, Barbados 0
Largest margin of victory, shutout: 8
  June 15, 2008; USA 8, Barbados 0
Largest margin of defeat: 11
  August 6, 1948; Norway 11, USA 0
Largest margin of defeat, shutout: 11
  August 6, 1948; Norway 11, USA 0

YEAR (TEAM RECORDS)

Most Games Played: 34 (1993)
Most wins: 16 (2013)
Most losses: 11 (1990)
Most ties: 11 (1993)
Most consecutive wins: 12 (2013)
Most consecutive losses: 5 (1975, 2007)

INDIVIDUAL RECORDS

Most goals: 4
  Archie Stark, November 8, 1925, vs. Canada
  Aldo Donelli, May 24, 1934, vs. Mexico

Joe-Max Moore, December 5, 1993, vs. El Salvador
Landon Donovan, July 19, 2003, vs. Cuba
Most assists: 3
Cobi Jones, November 14, 1993, vs. Cayman Islands
Landon Donovan, April 1, 2009, vs. Trinidad & Tobago
Landon Donovan, July 21, 2013, vs. El Salvador
Most points: 10
Joe-Max Moore, December 5, 1995, vs. El Salvador (4 goals, 2 assists)

YEAR (INDIVIDUAL RECORDS)

Most games played: 30
Cobi Jones, 1993
Most consecutive games: 21
Michael Windischmann, 1990
Marcelo Balboa, 1992
Most games started: 26
Chris Henderson, 1993
Most consecutive starts: 21
Marcelo Balboa, 1992
Most goals: 9
Eric Wynalda, 1996
Landon Donovan, 2007
Clint Dempsey, 2015
Most assists: 10
Landon Donovan, 2009
Most points: 24
Landon Donovan, 2013 (8 goals, 8 assists)
Most shutouts: 8
Kasey Keller, 2005

CAREER RECORDS

Most games played: 164
Cobi Jones, 1992–2004
Most consecutive games played: 36
Michael Windischmann, 1988–1990
Most consecutive games started: 33
Michael Windischmann, 1988–1990
Most consecutive appearances scoring a goal: 5
Jozy Altidore, 2013
Most consecutive appearances with an assist: 4
Landon Donovan, 2004, 2009

Most games started: 142
    Landon Donovan, 2000–2014
Most goals: 57
    Landon Donovan, 2000–2014
Most assists: 58
    Landon Donovan, 2000–2014
Most points: 172
    Landon Donovan, 2000–2014 (57 goals, 58 assists)
Most shutouts: 47
    Kasey Keller, 1990–2007

All records through December 31, 2016.
Source: U.S. Soccer.

Appendix B

U.S. Men's National Team World Cup Box Scores (1930–2014)

1930 WORLD CUP (URUGUAY)

July 13, 1930: USA 3–0 Belgium [HT 2–0]
Montevideo, Estadío Parque Central (10,000)
World Cup Finals (Uruguay) Round 1
Scorers: Bart McGhee 41', Tom Florie 45', Bert Patenaude 88'
USA: Jimmy Douglas, Alexander Wood, George Moorhouse, Jimmy Gallagher, Raphael Tracey, Billy Gonsalves, Andy Auld, James Brown, Bert Patenaude, Tom Florie, Bart McGhee
BEL: Arnold Badjou, Theodore Nouwens, Nico Hoydonckx, Pierre Braine, Gustav Hellemans, Jean de Clerq, Louis Versijp, Bernard Voorhoof, Ferdinand Adams, Jacques Moeschal, Jan Diddens

July 17, 1930: USA 3–0 Paraguay [HT 2–0]
Montevideo, Estadío Parque Central (20,800)
World Cup Finals (Uruguay) Round 1
Scorers: Bert Patenaude 10', Bert Patenaude 15', Bert Patenaude 50'
USA: Jimmy Douglas, Alexander Wood, George Moorhouse, Jimmy Gallagher, Raphael Tracey, Billy Gonsalves, Andy Auld, James Brown, Bert Patenaude, Tom Florie, Bart McGhee
PAR: Modesto Denis, Quiterio Olmedo, José Leon Miracca, Romildo Etcheverry, Eusebio Díaz, Francisco Aguirre, Lino Nessi, Diogenes Dominguez, Aurelio González, Delfin Benítez Caceres, Luis Vargas Pena

July 26, 1930: Argentina 6–1 USA [HT 1–0]
Montevideo, Estadío Centenario (80,000)
World Cup Finals (Uruguay) Seminfinal
Scorers: Luis Monti 20', Alejandro Scopelli 56', Guillermo Stabile 69',
   Guillermo Stabile 87', Carlos Peucelle 80', Carlos Peucelle 85'—James
   Brown 89'
ARG: Juan Botasso, José Della Torre, Fernando Paternoster, Juan Evaristo,
   Luis Monti, Rodolfo Orlandini, Carlos Peucelle, Alejandro Scopelli,
   Guillermo Stabile, Manuel Ferreira, Marino Evaristo
USA: Jimmy Douglas, Alexander Wood, George Moorhouse, Jimmy Gal-
   lagher, Raphael Tracey, Billy Gonsalves, Andy Auld, James Brown, Bert
   Patenaude, Tom Florie, Bart McGhee

1934 WORLD CUP (ITALY)

May 27, 1934: Italy 7–1 USA [HT 3–0]
Rome, Stadio Nazionale del PNF (30,000)
World Cup Finals (Italy) Round 1
Scorers: Angelo Schiavio 18', Angelo Schiavio 29', Angelo Schiavio 64',
   Raymundo Orsi 20', 69', Giovanni Ferrari 63', Giuseppe Meazza 90'—
   Aldo Donelli 57'
ITA: Giampiero Combi, Virginio Rosetta, Luigi Allemandi, Mario Pizzi-
   olo, Luis Monti, Luigi Bertolini, Anfilogino Guarisi, Giuseppe Meazza,
   Angelo Schiavio, Giovanni Ferrari, Raymundo Orsi
USA: Julius Hjulian, Ed Czerkiewicz, George Moorhouse, Peter Pietras,
   Billy Gonsalves, Tom Florie, Francis Ryan, Werner Nilsen, Aldo Do-
   nelli, Walter Dick, Bill McLean

1950 WORLD CUP (BRAZIL)

June 25, 1950: Spain 3–1 USA [HT 0–1]
Curitibia, Estadío Durival de Brito (9,511)
World Cup Finals (Brazil) Round 1
Scorers: Silvestre Igoa 54', Estanislao Basora 56', Zarra 63'—John Souza
   17'
ESP: Ignacio Eizaguirre, Gabriel Alonso, Francisco Antunez, José Gon-
   zalvo, Mariano Gonzalvo, Antonio Puchades, Estanislao Basora,
   Rosendo Hernández, Zarra, Silvestre Igoa, Agustin Gainza
USA: Frank Borghi, Harry Keough, Joe Maca, Eddie McIlvenny, Charlie
   Colombo, Walter Bahr, Adam Wolanin, Gino Pariani, Joe Gaetjens,
   John Souza, Frank Wallace

June 29, 1950: USA 1–0 England [HT 1–0]
Belo Horizonte, Estadío Independencia (10,151)
World Cup Finals (Brazil) Round 1
Scorer: Joe Gaetjens 38'
USA: Frank Borghi, Harry Keough, Joe Maca, Eddie McIlvenny, Charlie Colombo, Walter Bahr, Frank Wallace, Gino Pariani, Joe Gaetjens, John Souza, Ed Souza
ENG: Bert Williams, Alf Ramsey, John Aston, Billy Wright, Laurie Hughes, Jimmy Dickinson, Tom Finney, Stanley Mortensen, Roy Bentley, Wilf Mannion, Jimmy Mullen

July 2, 1950: Chile 5–2 USA [HT 2–0]
Recife, Estadío Esporte Clube Recife (8,501)
World Cup Finals (Brazil) Round 1
Scorers: George Robledo 16', Atillo Cremaschi 33', Atillo Cremaschi 60', Andres Prieto 54', Fernando Riera 82'—Gino Pariani 46', John Souza 49' (PK)
CHI: Sergio Livingstone, Arturo Farias, Manuel Alvarez, Manuel Machuca, Miguel Busquets, Carlos Rojas, Fernando Riera, Andres Prieto, Atillo Cremaschi, George Robledo, Carlos Ibanez
USA: Frank Borghi, Harry Keough, Joe Maca, Eddie McIlvenny, Charlie Colombo, Walter Bahr, Frank Wallace, Gino Pariani, Joe Gaetjens, John Souza, Ed Souza

1990 WORLD CUP (ITALY)

June 10, 1990: Czechoslovakia 5–1 USA [HT 2–0]
Florence, Stadio Comunale (33,266)
World Cup Finals (Italy) Group A
Scorers: Tomas Skuhravy 25', Michal Bilek 39' (PK), Ivan Hasek 50', Tomas Skuhravy 78', Milan Luhovy 90'—Paul Caligiuri 61'
TCH: Jan Stejskal, Frantisek Straka, Miroslav Kadlec, Jan Kocian, Ivan Hasek, Lubos Kubik, Michal Bilek, Jozef Chovanec, Lubomir Moravcik (Vladimir Weiss 83'), Tomas Skuhravy, Ivo Knoflicek (Milan Luhovy 77')
USA: Tony Meola, Steve Trittschuh, Michael Windischmann, John Harkes, Tab Ramos, Peter Vermes, Eric Wynalda, John Stollmeyer (Marcelo Balboa 64'), Desmond Armstrong, Bruce Murray (Christopher Sullivan 78'), Paul Caligiuri
Referee: Kurt Roethlisberger (SUI)
Cards: Lubos Kubik [Y 30'], Miroslav Kadlec [Y 61']—Tony Meola [Y 39'], Steve Trittschuh [Y 43'], Eric Wynalda [R 52']

June 14, 1990: Italy 1–0 USA [HT 1–0]
Rome, Stadio Olympico (73,423)
World Cup Finals (Italy) Group A
Scorer: Giuseppe Giannini 11'
ITA: Walter Zenga, Franco Baresi, Giuseppe Bergomi, Riccardo Ferri, Paolo Maldini, Nicola Berti, Fernando de Napoli, Giuseppe Giannini, Andrea Carnevale (Salvatore Schillaci 51'), Roberto Donadoni, Gianluca Vialli
USA: Tony Meola, John Doyle, Jimmy Banks (John Stollmeyer 80'), Michael Windischmann, John Harkes, Tab Ramos, Peter Vermes, Desmond Armstrong, Bruce Murray (Christopher Sullivan 82'), Marcelo Balboa, Paul Caligiuri
Referee: Edgardo Codesal Méndez (MEX)
Cards: Riccardo Ferri [Y 69']—Jimmy Banks [Y 62']

June 19, 1990: Austria 2–1 USA [HT 0–0]
Florence, Stadio Comunale (34,857)
World Cup Finals (Italy) Group A
Scorers: Andreas Ogris 49', Gerhard Rodax 63'—Bruce Murray 85'
AUT: Klaus Lindenberger, Ernst Aigner, Robert Pecl, Anton Artner, Michael Streiter, Manfred Zsak, Andreas Herzog, Andreas Ogris, Anton Polster (Andreas Reisinger 46'), Gerhard Rodax (Gerald Glatzmayer 84')
USA: Tony Meola, John Doyle, Jimmy Banks (Eric Wynalda 55'), Michael Windischmann, John Harkes, Tab Ramos, Peter Vermes, Desmond Armstrong, Bruce Murray, Marcelo Balboa, Paul Caligiuri (Brian Bliss 70')
Referee: Jamal Al-Sharif (SYR)
Cards: Manfred Zsak [Y 21'], Robert Pecl [Y 31'], Peter Artner [R 34'], Andreas Reisinger [Y 50'], Klaus Lindenberger [Y 84']—Paul Caligiuri [Y 26'], Jimmy Banks [Y 28'], Bruce Murray [Y 42']

1994 WORLD CUP (USA)

June 18, 1994: USA 1–1 Switzerland [HT 1–1]
Pontiac, Silver Dome (73,425)
World Cup Finals (USA) Group A
Scorers: Eric Wynalda 44'—Georges Bregy 39'
USA: Tony Meola, Cle Kooiman, Thomas Dooley, John Harkes, Earnie Stewart (Cobi Jones 81'), Tab Ramos, Eric Wynalda (Roy Wegerle 58'), Mike Sorber, Marcelo Balboa, Paul Caligiuri, Alexi Lalas
SUI: Marco Pascolo, Marc Hottiger, Yvan Quentin, Dominique Herr, Alain Geiger, Georges Bregy, Alain Sutter, Christophe Ohrel, Ciriaco

Sforza (Thomas Wyss 77'), Stephane Chapuisat, Thomas Bickel (Nestor Subiat 72')
Referee: Francisco Oscar Lamolina (ARG)
Cards: John Harkes [Y 89']—Dominique Herr [Y 26'], Nestor Subiat [Y 82']

June 22, 1994: USA 2–1 Colombia [HT 1–0]
Pasadena, Rose Bowl (93,689)
World Cup Finals (USA) Group A
Scorers: 'Earnie Stewart 52'—Andres Escobar 35' (OG), Adolfo Valencia 90'
USA: Tony Meola, Thomas Dooley, John Harkes, Earnie Stewart (Cobi Jones 66'), Tab Ramos, Eric Wynalda (Roy Wegerle 61'), Mike Sorber, Marcelo Balboa, Paul Caligiuri, Fernando Clavijo, Alexi Lalas
COL: Oscar Cordoba, Andres Escobar, Luis Herrera, Herman Gaviria, Anthony de Avila (Ivan Valenciano 46'), Carlos Valderrama, Leonel Alvarez, Luis Carlos Perea, Freddy Rincon, Wilson Perez, Faustino Asprilla (Adolfo Valencia 46')
Referee: Fabio Baldas (ITA)
Cards: Alexi Lalas [Y 48'], Anthony de Avila [Y 24']

June 26, 1994: USA 0–1 Romania [HT 0–1]
Pasadena, Rose Bowl (93,869)
World Cup Finals (USA) Group A
Scorer: Dan Petrescu 17'
USA: Tony Meola, Thomas Dooley, John Harkes, Earnie Stewart, Tab Ramos (Cobi Jones 64'), Eric Wynalda, Mike Sorber (Roy Wegerle 75'), Marcelo Balboa, Paul Caligiuri, Fernando Clavijo, Alexi Lalas
ROU: Florin Prunea, Dan Petrescu, Daniel Prodan, Miodrag Belodedici (Gheorghe Mihali 88'), Tibor Selymes, Dorinel Munteanu, Gica Popescu, Gheorghe Hagi, Ioan Lupescu, Ilie Dumitrescu, Florin Raducioiu (Constantin Galca 83')
Referee: Mario van der Ende (NED)
Cards: John Harkes [Y 41'], Fernando Clavijo [Y 48']—Florin Raducioiu [Y 62'], Dan Petrescu [Y 73']

July 4, 1994: USA 0–1 Brazil [HT 0–0]
Palo Alto, Stanford Stadium (84,147)
World Cup Finals (USA) Round 16
Scorer: Bebeto 72' (0–1)
USA: Tony Meola, Thomas Dooley, Hugo Pérez (Roy Wegerle 66'), Earnie Stewart, Tab Ramos (Eric Wynalda 46'), Cobi Jones, Mike Sorber, Marcelo Balboa, Paul Caligiuri, Fernando Clavijo, Alexi Lalas
BRA: Taffarel, Jorginho, Aldair, Márcio Santos, Leonardo, Mauro Silva, Dunga, Mazinho, Zinho (Cafu 69'), Bebeto, Romário

Referee: Joel Quiniou (FRA)
Cards: Tab Ramos [Y 43'], Paul Caligiuri [Y 49'], Fernando Clavijo [Y 64',R
    85'], Thomas Dooley [Y 80']—Mazinho [Y 8'], Jorginho [Y 16'], Leonardo
    [R 43']

1998 WORLD CUP (FRANCE)

June 15, 1998: Germany 2–0 USA [HT 1–0]
Paris, Parc des Princes (43,815)
World Cup Finals (France) Round 1, Group F
Scorers: Andreas Möller 8', Jurgen Klinsmann 65'
GER: Andreas Köpke, Christian Worns, Jurgen Kohler, Olaf Thon, Jens
    Jeremies, Stefan Reuter (Christian Ziege 68'), Andreas Möller (Markus
    Babbel 86'), Thomas Hassler (Dietmar Hamann 50'), Jorg Heinrich, Oli-
    ver Bierhoff, Jurgen Klinsmann
USA: Kasey Keller, Thomas Dooley, Eddie Pope, David Regis, Cobi Jones,
    Mike Burns (Frankie Hejduk 46'), Chad Deering (Tab Ramos 70'), Brian
    Maisonneuve, Earnie Stewart, Claudio Reyna, Eric Wynalda (Roy We-
    gerle 65')
Cards: Jens Jeremies [Y 30'], Dietmar Hamann [Y 77'], Jorg Heinrich [Y
    84']—Frankie Hejduk [Y 50'], Eddie Pope [Y 85']

June 21, 1998: Iran 2–1 USA [HT 1–0]
Lyon, Stade Gerland (44,000)
World Cup (France) Group F
Scorers: Hamid Reza Estili 40', Mehdi Mahdavikia 84'—Brian McBride 87'
IRN: Ahmedreza Abedzadeh, Mehdi Mahdavikia, Mohammad Khak-
    pour, Hamid Reza Estili, Javad Zarincheh (Naim Saadavi 77'), Nader
    Mohammadkhani (Mohammad Peyrovani 74'), Mehdi Pashazadeh,
    Mehrdad Minavand, Karim Bagheri, Ali Daei, Khodadad Azizi (Ali
    Reza Mansourian 73')
USA: Kasey Keller, Frankie Hejduk, Eddie Pope, Thomas Dooley (Brian
    Maisonneuve 82'), David Regis, Roy Wegerle (Predrag Radosavljevic
    57'), Joe-Max Moore, Tab Ramos (Earnie Stewart 57'), Cobi Jones, Brian
    McBride, Claudio Reyna
Cards: Mehrdad Minavand [Y 8'], Javad Zarincheh [Y 77']—David Regis
    [Y 18']

June 25, 1998: Yugoslavia 1–0 USA [HT 1–0]
Nantes, Stade la Beaujoire (39,500)
World Cup (France) Group F
Scorer: Slobodan Komljenovic 4'

YUG: Ivica Kralj, Goran Djorovic, Slobodan Komljenovic, Zeljko Petrovic, Slavisa Jokanovic, Vladimir Jugovic, Dragan Stojkovic (Dejan Savicevic 62'), Sinisa Mihajlovic, Dejan Stankovic (Branko Brnovic 55'), Predrag Mijatovic (Perica Ognjenovic 31'), Savo Milosevic

USA: Brad Friedel, David Regis, Frankie Hejduk (Eric Wynalda 64'), Thomas Dooley (Marcelo Balboa 82'), Mike Burns, Cobi Jones, Claudio Reyna, Brian Maisonneuve, Joe-Max Moore (Predrag Radosavljevic 58'), Brian McBride, Earnie Stewart

Cards: Dejan Stankovic [Y 41'], Perica Ognjenovic [Y 61']—Claudio Reyna [Y 13']

2002 WORLD CUP (SOUTH KOREA/JAPAN)

June 5, 2002: USA 3–2 Portugal [HT 3–1]
Suwon, Suwon Stadium (37,306)
World Cup (South Korea) Group D
Scorers: John O'Brien (Brian McBride) 4', Brian McBride (Tony Sanneh) 36', Jeff Agoos (OG) 71'—Jorge Costa 30' (OG), 'Beto (unassisted) 39'

USA: 1-Brad Friedel, 2-Frankie Hejduk, 12-Jeff Agoos, 23-Eddie Pope (16-Carlos Llamosa 80'), 22-Tony Sanneh, 4-Pablo Mastroeni, 17-DaMarcus Beasley, 5-John O'Brien, 8-Earnie Stewart (capt.; 13-Cobi Jones 46'); 21-Landon Donovan (9-Joe-Max Moore 75'), 20-Brian McBride

POR: 1-Vitor Baia, 2-Jorge Costa (13-Jorge Andrade 73'), 5-Fernando Couto (capt.), 23-Rui Jorge (17-Paulo Bento 69'), 20-Petit, 10-Rui Costa (21-Nuno Gomes 80'), 11-Sergio Conceicao, 22-Beto, 7-Luis Figo, 9-Pauleta, 8-Joao Pinto

Referee: Bryon Moreno (ECU)
Cards: DaMarcus Beasley [Y 90+2']—Beto [Y 14'], Petit [Y 52']

June 10, 2002: South Korea 1–1 USA [HT 0–1]
Daegu, Daegu Stadium (60,778)
World Cup (South Korea) Group D
Scorers: Lee Eul-Yong 40', Ahn Jung-Hwan 78'—Clint Mathis 24'

KOR: 1-Lee Woon-Jae; 4-Choi Jin-Chul, 5-Kim Nam-Il, 6-Yoo Sang-Chul (11-Choi Yong-Soo 69'), 7-Kim Tae-Young, 9-Seol Ki-Hyun, 13-Lee Eul-Yong, 18-Hwang Sun-Hong (19-Ahn Jung-Hwan 56'), 20-Hong Myung-Bo (capt.), 21-Park Ji-Sung (14-Lee Chun-Soo 38'), 22-Song Chong-Gug

USA: 1-Brad Friedel, 2-Frankie Hejduk, 5-John O'Brien, 10-Claudio Reyna (capt.), 11-Clint Mathis (15-Josh Wolff 83'), 12-Jeff Agoos, 17-DaMarcus Beasley (7-Eddie Lewis 75'), 20-Brian McBride, 21-Landon Donovan, 22-Tony Sanneh, 23-Eddie Pope

Referee: Urs Meier (SUI)
Cards: Frankie Hejduk [Y 30'], Jeff Agoos [Y 39'], Hong Myung-bo [Y 80']

June 14, 2002: Poland 3–1 USA [HT 2–0]
Daejeon, Daejoen Stadium (26,482)
World Cup (South Korea) Group D
Scorers: Emmanuel Olisadebe (unassisted) 3', Pawel Kryszalowicz (Jacek Kryznowek) 5', Marcin Zewlakow (n/a) 66'—Landon Donovan (Clint Mathis) 83'
POL: 12-Radoslaw Madjan, 2-Tomasz Klos (15 Tomasz Waldoch 89'), 3-Jacek Zielinski (capt.), 13-Arkadiusz Glowacki, 21-Marek Kozminski, 19-Maciej Zurawski, 16-Maciej Murawski, 18-Jacek Krzynowek, 8-Cezary Kucharski (14-Marcin Zewlakow 65'), 9-Pawel Kryszalowicz, 11-Emmanuel Olisadebe (23-Pawel Sibik 86')
USA: 1-Brad Friedel, 2-Frankie Hejduk, 12-Jeff Agoos (17-DaMarcus Beasley 36'), 23-Eddie Pope, 22-Tony Sanneh, 10-Claudio Reyna (capt.), 8-Earnie Stewart (13-Cobi Jones 68'), 5-John O'Brien, 21-Landon Donovan, 11-Clint Mathis, 20-Brian McBride (9-Joe-Max Moore 58')
Referee: Lu Jun (CHN)
Cards: Radoslaw Madjan [Y 44'], Marek Kozminski [Y 46'], Cezary Kucharski [Y 63'], Emmanuel Olisadebe [Y 86']—Frankie Hejduk [Y 72']

June 17, 2002: USA 2–0 Mexico [HT 1–0]
Jeonju, Jeonju Stadium (36,380)
World Cup (South Korea) Round 16
Scorers: Brian McBride (Josh Wolff) 8', Landon Donovan (Eddie Lewis) 65'
USA: 1-Brad Friedel, 3-Gregg Berhalter, 23-Eddie Pope, 22-Tony Sanneh, 4-Pablo Mastroeni (16-Carlos Llamosa 92+'), 7-Eddie Lewis, 10-Claudio Reyna (capt.), 5-John O'Brien, 21-Landon Donovan, 20-Brian McBride (13-Cobi Jones 79'), 15-Josh Wolff (8-Earnie Stewart 59')
MEX: 1-Oscar Perez, 16-Salvador Carmona, 4-Rafael Marquez (capt.), 5-Manuel Vidrio (13-Sigifredo Mercado 46'), 7-Ramon Morales (15-Luis Hernandez 28'), 11-Braulio Luna, 18-Joahan Rodriguez, 6-Gerardo Torrado (8-Alberto Garcia Aspe 78'), 21-Jesus Arellano, 10-Cuauhtemoc Blanco, 9-Jared Borgetti
Referee: Vitor Melo Pereira (POR)
Cards: Eddie Pope [Y 26'], Pablo Mastroeni [Y 47'], Josh Wolff [Y 50'], Gregg Berhalter [Y 53'], Brad Friedel [Y 83']—Manuel Vidrio [Y 37'], Luis Hernandez [Y 67'], Cuauhtemoc Blanco [Y 70'], Alberto Garcia Aspe [Y 81'], Salvador Carmona [Y 84'], Rafael Marquez [R 88']

June 21, 2002: Germany 1–0 USA [HT 1–0]
Ulsan, Munsu Stadium, 37,337
World Cup (South Korea) Quarterfinals
Scorer: Michael Ballack (Christian Ziege) 39'
GER: 1-Oliver Kahn (capt.), 21-Christoph Metzelder, 15-Sebastian Kehl, 2-Thomas Linke, 19-Bernd Schneider (16-Jans Jeremies 60'), 8-Dietmar Hamann, 6-Christian Ziege, 22-Torsten Frings, 13-Michael Ballack, 7-Oliver Neuville (17-Marco Bode 80'), 11-Miroslav Klose (20-Oliver Bierhoff 88')
USA: 1-Brad Friedel, 3-Gregg Berhalter, 23-Eddie Pope, 22-Tony Sanneh, 4-Pablo Mastroeni (8-Earnie Stewart 80'), 7-Eddie Lewis, 10-Claudio Reyna (capt.), 2-Frankie Hejduk (13-Cobi Jones 65'), 5-John O'Brien, 21-Landon Donovan, 20-Brian McBride (11-Clint Mathis 58')
Referee: Hugh Dallas (SCO)
Cards: Sebastian Kehl [Y 66'], Oliver Neuville [Y 68']—Eddie Lewis [Y 40'], Eddie Pope [Y 41'], Claudio Reyna [Y 68'], Pablo Mastroeni [Y 69'], Gregg Berhalter[Y 70']

2006 WORLD CUP (GERMANY)

June 12, 2006: USA 0–3 Czech Republic [HT 0–2]
Gelsenkirchen, FIFA World Cup Stadium Gelsenkirchen (52,000)
World Cup (Germany) Group E
Scorers: Jan Koller (Zdenek Grygera) 5', Tomas Rosicky (unassisted) 36', Tomas Rosicky (Pavel Nedved) 76'
USA: 18-Kasey Keller, 6-Steve Cherundolo (9-Eddie Johnson 46'), 23-Eddie Pope, 22-Oguchi Onyewu, 7-Eddie Lewis, 17-DaMarcus Beasley, 10-Claudio Reyna, 4-Pablo Mastroeni (5-John O'Brien 46'), 15-Bobby Convey, 21-Landon Donovan, 20-Brian McBride (16-Josh Wolff 77'). Head Coach: Bruce Arena
CZE: 1-Petr Cech, 2-Zdenek Grygera, 21-Tomas Ujfalusi, 22-David Rozehnal, 6-Marek Jankulovski, 8-Karel Poborksi (19-Jan Polak 82'), 10-Tomas Rosicky (17-Jiri Stajner 86'), 4-Tomas Galasek, 11-Pavel Nedved, 20-Jaroslav Plasil, 9-Jan Koller (12-Vratislav Lokvenc 45'). Head Coach: Karel Bruckner
Referee: Carlos Amarilla (PAR)
Cards: Oguchi Onyewu [Y 5'], Claudio Reyna [Y 60']—David Rozehal [Y 16'], Vratislav Lokvenc [Y 59'], Tomas Rosicky [Y 81'], Zdenek Grygera [Y 88']

June 17, 2006: USA 1–1 Italy [HT 1–1]
Kaiserslautern, Fritz-Walter Stadion (46,000)

World Cup (Germany) Group E

Scorers: Cristian Zaccardo (own goal) 27', Alberto Gilardino (Andrea Pirlo) 22'

USA: 18-Kasey Keller, 6-Steve Cherundolo, 23-Eddie Pope, 22-Oguchi Onyewu, 3-Carlos Bocanegra, 4-Pablo Mastroeni, 8-Clint Dempsey (17-DaMarcus Beasley 62'), 10-Claudio Reyna (capt.), 15-Bobby Convey (13-Jimmy Conrad 52'), 21-Landon Donovan, 20-Brian McBride. Head Coach: Bruce Arena

ITA: 1-Gianluigi Buffon, 2-Cristian Zaccardo (7-Alessandro del Piero 54'), 5-Fabio Cannavaro (capt.), 13-Alessandro Nesta, 19-Gianluca Zambrotto, 4-Daniele De Rossi, 20-Simone Perrotta, 21-Andrea Pirlo, 10-Francesco Totti (8-Gennaro Gattuso 35'), 11-Alberto Gilardino, 9-Luca Toni (15-Vincenzo Iaquinta 61'). Head Coach: Marcello Lippi

Referee: Jorge Larrionda (URU)

Cards: Eddie Pope [Y 21', 47'], Pablo Mastroeni [R 45']—Francesco Totti [Y 5'], Daniele De Rossi [R 28'], Gianluca Zambrotto [Y 70']

June 22, 2006: USA 1–2 Ghana [HT 1–2]
Nuremberg, Frankenstadion (41,000)
World Cup (Germany) Group E

Scorers: Clint Dempsey (DaMarcus Beasley) 43'—Haminu Draman (unassisted) 22', Stephen Appiah (PK) 47+'

USA: 18-Kasey Keller, 6-Steve Cherundolo (9-Eddie Johnson 61'), 13-Jimmy Conrad, 22-Oguchi Onyewu, 3-Carlos Bocanegra, 10-Claudio Reyna (14-Ben Olsen 40'), 8-Clint Dempsey, 21-Landon Donovan, 17-DaMarcus Beasley, 7-Eddie Lewis (15-Bobby Convey 74'), 20-Brian McBride. Head Coach: Bruce Arena

GHA: 22-Richard Kingson, 15-John Pantsil, 5-John Mensah, 13-Habib Mohamed, 7-Illiasu Shilla, 8-Michael Essien, 9-Derek Boateng (20-Otto Addo 46'), 10-Stephen Appiah, 23-Haminu Draman (12-Alex Tachie-Mensah 80'); 14-Matthew Amoah (18-Eric Addo 59'), 19-Razak Pimpong. Head Coach: Ratomir Dujkovic

Referee: Markus Merk (GER)

Cards: Eddie Lewis [Y 7']—Michael Essien [Y 5'], Illiasu Shilla [Y 32'], John Mensah [Y 81'], Stephen Appiah [Y 91+']

2010 WORLD CUP (SOUTH AFRICA)

June 12, 2010: USA 1–1 England [HT 1–1]
Rustenburg, Royal Bafokeng Stadium (38,646)
World Cup (South Africa) Group C

Scorers: Clint Dempsey (unassisted) 40'—Steven Gerrard (Emile Heskey) 4'

USA: 1-Tim Howard, 6-Steve Cherundolo, 15-Jay DeMerit, 5-Oguchi Onyewu, 3-Carlos Bocanegra (capt.), 10-Landon Donovan, 13-Ricardo Clark, 4-Michael Bradley, 8-Clint Dempsey, 20-Robbie Findley (14-Edson Buddle 77'), 17-Jozy Altidore (11-Stuart Holden 86'). Head Coach: Bob Bradley

ENG: 12-Robert Green, 2-Glen Johnson, 6-John Terry, 20-Ledley King (18-Jamie Carragher 46'), 3-Ashley Cole, 7-Aaron Lennon, 8-Frank Lampard, 4-Steven Gerrard (capt.), 16-James Milner (Shaun Wright-Phillips 31'), 10-Wayne Rooney, 21-Emile Heskey (9-Peter Crouch 79'). Head Coach: Fabio Capello

Referee: Carlos Simon (BRA)

Cards: Steve Cherundolo [Y 39'], Jay DeMerit [Y 47'], Robbie Findley [Y 74']—James Milner [Y 26'], Jamie Carragher [Y 60'], Steven Gerrard [Y 61']

June 18, 2010 USA 2–2 Slovenia [HT 0–2]
Johannesburg, Ellis Park (45,573)
World Cup (South Africa) Group C

Scorers: Landon Donovan (Steve Cherundolo) 48', Michael Bradley (Jozy Altidore) 82'—Valter Birsa (unassisted) 13', Zlatan Ljubijankic (Milivoje Novakovic) 42'

USA: 1-Tim Howard, 6-Steve Cherundolo, 15-Jay DeMerit, 5-Oguchi Onyewu (9-Herculez Gomez 80'), 3-Carlos Bocanegra, 8-Clint Dempsey, 4-Michael Bradley, 16-Jose Torres (19-Maurice Edu 46'), 10-Landon Donovan, 20-Robbie Findley (22-Benny Feilhaber 46'), 17-Jozy Altidore. Head Coach: Bob Bradley

SVN: 1-Samir Handanovic, 2-Miso Brecko, 4-Marko Suler, 5-Bostjan Cesar, 13-Bojan Jokic, 8-Robert Koren (capt.), 9-Zlatan Ljubijankic (7-Nejc Pecnik 74'), 20-Andrej Komac (90+4'), 10-Valter Birsa (14-Zlatko Dedic 87'), 17-Andraz Kirm, 18-Aleksandar Radosavljevic, 11-Milivoje Novakovic. Head Coach: Matjaz Kek

Referee: Koman Coulibaly (MLI)

Cards: Robbie Findley [Y 40']—Bostjan Cesar [Y 35'], Marko Suler [Y 69'], Andraz Kirm [Y 72'], Bojan Jokic [Y 75']

June 23, 2010: USA 1–0 Algeria [HT 0–0]
Pretoria, Loftus Versfeld Stadium (35,827)
World Cup (South Africa) Group C

Scorer: Landon Donovan (unassisted) 90+1'

USA: 1-Tim Howard, 6-Steve Cherundolo, 15-Jay DeMerit, 3-Carlos Bocanegra (capt.), 12-Jonathan Bornstein (7-DaMarcus Beasley 80'), 10-Landon Donovan, 4-Michael Bradley, 19-Maurice Edu (14-Edson

Buddle 64'), 8-Clint Dempsey, 9-Herculez Gomez (22-Benny Feilhaber 46'), 17-Jozy Altidore. Head Coach: Bob Bradley

ALG: 23-Raïs M'Bohli, 2-Madjid Bougherra, 3-Nadir Belhadj, 4-Anthar Yahia (capt.), 5-Rafik Halliche, 8-Mehdi Lacen, 13-Karim Matmour (10-Rafik Saifi 85'), 15-Karim Ziani (17-Adlane Guedioura 69'), 19-Hassan Yebda, 11-Rafik Djebbour (9-Abdelkader Ghezzal 65'), 21-Foued Kadir. Head Coach: Rabah Saadane

Referee: Frank De Bleeckere (BEL)

Cards: Jozy Altidore [Y 62'], DaMarcus Beasley [Y 90']—Hassan Yebda [Y 12'], Anthar Yahia [Y 76', 90+3'], Mehdi Lacen [Y 83']

June 26, 2010: USA 1–2 Ghana [HT 0–1]
Rustenburg, Royal Bafokeng Stadium (34,976)
World Cup (South Africa) Round 16

Scorers: Landon Donovan (PK) 62'—Kevin-Prince Boateng (unassisted) 5', Asamoah Gyan (Andre Ayew) 93'

USA: 1-Tim Howard, 6-Steve Cherundolo, 15-Jay DeMerit, 3-Carlos Bocanegra (capt.), 12-Jonathan Bornstein, 10-Landon Donovan, 4-Michael Bradley, 13-Ricardo Clark (19-Maurice Edu 31'), 8-Clint Dempsey, 20-Robbie Findley (22-Benny Feilhaber 46'), 17-Jozy Altidore (9-Herculez Gomez 91'). Head Coach: Bob Bradley

GHA: 22-Richard Kingson, 2-Hans Sarpei (19-Lee Addy 73'), 4-John Pantsil, 5-John Mensah (capt.), 7-Samuel Inkoom (11-Sulley Muntari 113'), 8-Jonathan Mensah, 6-Anthony Annan, 13-Andre Ayew, 21-Kwando Asamoah, 23-Kevin-Prince Boateng (10-Stephen Appiah 78'), 3-Asamoah Gyan. Head Coach: Milovan Rajevac

Referee: Viktor Kassai (HUN)

Cards: Ricardo Clark [Y 7'], Steve Cherundolo [Y 18'], Carlos Bocanegra [Y 68']—Jonathan Mensah [Y 61'], Andre Ayew [Y 90+2']

2014 WORLD CUP (BRAZIL)

June 16, 2014: Ghana 1–2 USA [HT 0–1]
Natal, Estadio das Dunas (39,760)
World Cup (Brazil) Group G

Scorers: Andre Ayew (Asamoah Gyan) 82'—Clint Dempsey (Jermaine Jones) 1', John Brooks (Graham Zusi) 86'

GHA: 12-Adam Kwarasey, 4-Daniel Opare, 19-Jonathan Mensah, 21-John Boye, 20-Kwadwo Asamoah, 17-Mohammed Rabiu (5-Michael Essien 71'), 7-Christian Atsu (14-Albert Adomah 78'), 11-Sulley Muntari, 13-Jordan Ayew (9-Kevin-Prince Boateng 59'), 3-Asamoah Gyan (capt.), 10-Andre Ayew

USA: 1-Tim Howard, 23-Fabian Johnson, 20-Geoff Cameron, 5-Matt Besler (6-John Brooks 46'), 7-DaMarcus Beasley, 11-Alejandro Bedoya (19-Graham Zusi 77'), 15-Kyle Beckerman, 13-Jermaine Jones, 4-Michael Bradley, 8-Clint Dempsey (capt.), 17-Jozy Altidore (9-Aron Johannsson 23'). Head Coach: Jurgen Klinsmann
Referee: Jonas Erikkson (SWE)
Cards: Mohammed Rabiu [Y 30'], Sulley Muntari [Y 90+2']

June 22, 2014: USA 2–2 Portugal [HT 0–1]
Manaus, Arena Amazonia (40,123)
World Cup (Brazil) Group G
Scorers: Jermaine Jones 64', Clint Dempsey (Graham Zusi) 81'—Nani (unassisted) 5', Silvestre Varela (Cristiano Ronaldo) 90+5'
USA: 1-Tim Howard, 23-Fabian Johnson, 20-Geoff Cameron, 5-Matt Besler, 7-DaMarcus Beasley, 15-Kyle Beckerman, 13-Jermaine Jones, 11-Alejandro Bedoya (2-DeAndre Yedlin 72'), 4-Michael Bradley, 19-Graham Zusi (3-Omar Gonzalez 90+1'), 8-Clint Dempsey (capt.) (18-Chris Wondolowski 87'). Head Coach: Jurgen Klinsmann
POR: 22-Beto, 2-Bruno Alves, 13-Ricardo Costa, 19-Andre Almeida (6-William Carvalho 46'), 21-Joao Pereira, 4-Miguel Veloso, 8-Joao Moutinho, 16-Raul Meireles (18-Silvestre Varela 69'), 7-Cristiano Ronaldo (capt.), 17-Nani, 23-Heider Postiga (11-Eder 16'). Head Coach: Paulo Bento
Referee: Nestor Pitana (ARG)
Cards: Jermaine Jones [Y 75']

June 26, 2014: USA 0–1 Germany [HT 0–0]
Recife, Arena Pernambuco (41,876)
World Cup (Brazil) Group G
Scorer: Thomas Muller (unassisted) 55'
USA: 1-Tim Howard, 23-Fabian Johnson, 3-Omar Gonzalez, 5-Matt Besler, 7-DaMarcus Beasley, 15-Kyle Beckerman, 13-Jermaine Jones, 14-Brad Davis (11-Alejandro Bedoya 59'), 4-Michael Bradley, 19-Graham Zusi (2-DeAndre Yedlin 84'), 8-Clint Dempsey (capt.). Head Coach: Jurgen Klinsmann
GER: 1-Manuel Neuer, 4-Benedikt Howedes, 5-Mats Hummels, 17-Per Mertesacker, 20-Jerome Boateng, 7-Bastian Schweinsteiger (19-Mario Gotze 76'), 16-Phillip Lahm, 18-Toni Kroos, 8-Mesut Ozil (9-Andre Schurrle 89'), 10-Lukas Podolski (11-Miroslav Klose 46'), 13-Thomas Muller. Head Coach: Joachim Löw
Referee: Ravshan Irmatov (UZB)
Cards: Omar Gonzalez [Y 37'], Kyle Beckerman [Y 62']—Benedikt Howedes [Y 11']

July 1, 2014: Belgium 2–1 USA [HT 0–0]
Salvador, Estadio Fonte Nova (51,227)
World Cup (Brazil) Round 16
Scorers: Kevin De Bruyne (unassisted) 93', Romelu Lukaku (Kevin De Bruyne) 105'—Julian Green (Michael Bradley) 107'
BEL: 1-Thibaut Courtois, 2-Toby Alderweireld, 4-Vincent Kompany (capt.), 5-Jan Vertonghen, 15-Daniel Van Buyten, 6-Axel Witsel, 7-Kevin De Bruyne, 8-Marouane Fellaini, 10-Eden Hazard (22-Nacer Chadli 111'), 14-Dries Mertens (11-Kevin Mirallas 60'), 17-Divock Origi (9-Romelu Lukaku 91'). Head Coach: Marc Wilmots
USA: 1-Tim Howard, 23-Fabian Johnson (2-DeAndre Yedlin 32'), 3-Omar Gonzalez, 5-Matt Besler, 7-DaMarcus Beasley, 20-Geoff Cameron, 4-Michael Bradley, 13-Jermaine Jones, 11-Alejandro Bedoya (16-Julian Green 105+2'), 8-Clint Dempsey (capt.), 19-Graham Zusi (18-Chris Wondolowski 72'). Head Coach: Jurgen Klinsmann
Referee: Djamel Haimoudi (ALG)
Cards: Vincent Kompany [Y 42']—Geoff Cameron [Y 18']

Compiled by Ed Farnsworth for the Society for American Soccer History.
To see every box score for every U.S. game, visit www.ussoccerhistory.org.

Bibliography

American Soccer History Archives
Boston Globe
Brooklyn Daily Eagle
Cirino, Tony. *U.S. Soccer vs. the World*. New York: Damon Press, 1983.
FIFA.com
Glanville, Brian. *The Story of the World Cup*. London: Faber & Faber, 2006.
The Guardian
Los Angeles Times
MLSSoccer.com
New York Times
Philadelphia Inquirer
SoccerAmerica.com
Society for American Soccer History
Sporting News
St. Louis Post-Dispatch
Staten Island Advance
Univision.com
USSoccer.com
Wangerin, Dave. *Soccer in a Football World*. Philadelphia, PA: Temple University Press, 2008.

Index

About the Author

Clemente A. Lisi has worked as a writer and editor for almost 20 years. His work has appeared in such newspapers as the *New York Post* and *New York Daily News*, and on websites like ABCNews.com and USSoccerPlayers.com. He lives in Brooklyn, New York, with his wife and two children.